363.3
G

KNOX TRAIL REG JHS

Gun control.

351359

W9-BXD-351

DATE DUE

APR 26 07			
GAYLORD			PRINTED IN U.S.A.

Open for Debate

Gun Control

Open for Debate

Gun Control

Susan Dudley Gold

BENCHMARK BOOKS

MARSHALL CAVENDISH
NEW YORK

KNOX TRAIL
LIBRARY

Thanks to Gregg L. Carter, Ph.D., professor of
sociology and Chair, Department of History and Social Sciences,
Bryant College, for his expert review of this manuscript.

Copyright © 2004 by Marshall Cavendish Corporation
Charts copyright © 2004 by Marshall Cavendish Corporation
All rights reserved. No part of this book may be reproduced or utilized in any form or
by any means electronic or mechanical including photocopying, recording, or by any
information storage and retrieval system, without permission from the copyright holders.

All Internet sites were available and accurate when sent to press.

Library of Congress Cataloging-in-Publication Data
Gold, Susan Dudley.
Gun control / by Susan Dudley Gold.
p. cm.— (Open for debate)
Summary: Discusses the history of guns and gun control in
the United States, relevant laws and legal cases, and the arguments
posed by both sides in the debate about how much government control there
should be over firearms. Includes bibliographical references and index.
ISBN 0-7614-1584-X
1. Gun control—United States. 2. Firearms ownership—United States.
3. Firearms—Law and legislation—United States. [1. Gun control. 2.
Firearms ownership. 3. Firearms—Law and legislation.] I. Title. II. Series.
HV7436.G65 2004
363.3'3'0973—dc21
2002155978

Photo research by Linda Sykes Picture Research, Hilton Head, South Carolina

Steven Rubin/The Image Works: Cover, 2–3, 5, 6; Reuters NewMedia Inc./Corbis: 8. 98;
Bettmann/Corbis: 28; Michael Freeman/Corbis: 35; Corbis: 42, 56; AFP/Corbis: 70, 93;
Bob Daemmrich/The Image Works: 112; Joe Skipper/Reuters/Getty Images: 113.

Printed in China

1 3 5 6 4 2

Contents

1
Snipers Take Aim

Thirteen-year-old Iran Brown had just stepped out of his aunt's car and was walking toward his school in Bowie, Maryland, when a bullet struck him in the abdomen. The October 7, 2002, shooting nearly killed Iran. He survived, but doctors had to remove his spleen and parts of his stomach and pancreas.

Iran was one of thirteen victims hit by a sniper's bullet during a three-week shooting spree that terrorized people living near the nation's capital. The snipers took deadly aim at men and women in Maryland, Virginia, and Washington, D.C., as they shopped, pumped gasoline, or did other daily chores.

Not until October 24, when police arrested forty-one-year-old John Allen Muhammad and seventeen-year-old Lee Boyd Malvo, did the fear subside. The accused snipers were linked not only to these thirteen attacks but to eight other shootings in Alabama, Louisiana, Washington, and Georgia. In all, the two were suspected of shooting fifteen people to

MONTGOMERY COUNTY POLICE CHIEF CHARLES MOOSE SHOWS IMAGES OF TWO VANS THAT POLICE THOUGHT MIGHT BE INVOLVED IN SNIPER SHOOTINGS IN THE WASHINGTON, D.C., AREA IN OCTOBER 2002. AS IT TURNED OUT, NEITHER WAS INVOLVED. THE TERRIFYING SHOOTING SPREE LED TO CALLS FOR A NATIONAL RECORD SYSTEM CAPABLE OF TRACKING BULLETS USED IN CRIMES.

death and wounding six others. Both were in jail waiting for court hearings on the charges when this book was written.

Police said that the bullets which had pierced the bodies of the victims came from a semiautomatic assault rifle found in the suspects' car. Muhammad's police record and Malvo's youth made it illegal for either of them to own the rifle. Malvo, a citizen of Jamaica, was actually doubly banned from owning a gun—he had entered the country illegally, according to police.

Spotlight on Gun Control

The D.C.-area sniper attacks fired up the already heated debate over gun control in the United States. Those in favor of gun control said the attacks showed the need for stronger gun laws. "Sensible gun laws can help law enforcement solve crimes as well as prevent gun violence," said Sarah Brady, chair of the Brady Campaign to Prevent Gun Violence, a national gun-control group.

For instance, Brady and others noted, a national "ballistic-fingerprint" record system could have helped police track the killers sooner. Under such a system, manufacturers would fire a bullet from each gun they produced, save the bullet, and record the unique pattern made by the gun barrel. If the system had been in effect during the D.C. sniper attacks, police might have been able to trace the gun and find the shooters earlier.

"If we are going to enforce the law, we need to ensure that our police officers have the best tools for the job. People's lives are at stake, and we need to support law enforcement efforts to solve gun crimes," said Michael D. Barnes, president of the Brady Campaign.

Gun-control advocates called for other measures as well. Background checks for all gun sales would keep more weapons out of the hands of criminals, they said. They also said that the assault rifle which the police believed the snipers had used should be banned from sale to anyone but police. It had been altered so that it did not fall under the assault-weapons ban in effect at the time of the shootings. Noting that the ban was scheduled to expire in 2004, Sarah Brady urged Congress to extend and expand the law to include more weapons.

Those against gun control expressed starkly different views of precisely what the sniper attacks demonstrated. They said the shootings showed that gun-control laws simply do not work. Criminals, they argued, can always find ways to obtain guns illegally. Police at the time were still trying to find out how Muhammad got the gun used in the shootings. Not until after Muhammad's arrest did a Seattle gun store owner report the gun stolen. An earlier government investigation had revealed that guns at the store were often stolen or misplaced.

Wayne LaPierre, executive vice president of the National Rifle Association (NRA), the country's leading gun-rights organization, issued statements against the proposal to set up a ballistic-fingerprint record system. "This scheme is a national gun registration and certain to produce confusion, misidentification and wrongful suspicion," LaPierre wrote. Gun-rights supporters have long held that if the government knows who owns guns, it can use that information to unjustly control and suppress its people. Furthermore, they claim, more gun controls would make it harder for law-abiding citizens to buy guns to protect themselves against attacks by criminals. "The answer to the gun problem is putting guns in the hands of responsible citizens, not taking them away from them," a gun-rights advocate told reporter Judy Woodruff during a news report on the shootings.

A Century-old Argument

Guns in the wrong hands can disable and kill innocent people and aid criminals. Guns in the right hands can save lives and prevent crime. These two statements seem straightforward enough.

But for more than a century, Americans who believe one of those statements have been unable to see the other side.

People on both sides of the argument know that the stakes are high. Thousands of Americans die each year from gun-inflicted injuries. According to the latest figures available from the federal government's National Vital Statistics Reports, 11,001 people were murdered with a firearm in 2001. Another 924 died as the result of accidental shootings. An additional 16,455 people used guns to kill themselves.

Firearms claim more lives in the United States than any other injury except motor vehicle accidents. In three states and the District of Columbia, gun-related incidents are the leading cause of death.

As frightening as the figures are, the rate of gun deaths has steadily declined in recent years. Each year since 1993, fewer Americans have died from gunshot wounds (although the number of homicides by gun rose slightly in 2001). Experts give varying reasons for the decline. These include:

- **a decrease in the number of people owning guns;**
- **a police crackdown on criminals;**
- **tougher jail terms for those using guns to commit crimes;**
- **a reduction in crack cocaine traffic;**
- **efforts to educate children and adults about gun safety;**
- **gun-control laws that have helped make it harder to get firearms;**
- **gun safety measures (for example, safety locks);**
- **fewer guns being manufactured.**

Alongside guns' obvious connection to death is their connection to crime. The Justice Department reports that almost 500,000 crimes involving guns are committed each year. According to some noted researchers, the figure may in fact be much higher—as many as 900,000 gun crimes annually. The lower figure represents the number of crimes reported to police, while the higher figure is based on estimates from surveys of crime victims.

Complicating the issue is the fact that guns are also used to protect against crime. Police and other law-enforcement officials use guns to apprehend criminals and stop them from committing further offenses. Private citizens, too, use guns to defend themselves and their property. U.S. government figures report that, by using guns, ordinary citizens prevent about 100,000 crimes each year. Other researchers put the figure much higher.

Violence around the World

In one year, murderers shot and killed:

165 people in Canada (1999 figures);
21,898 people in Colombia (2000 figures);
62 people in England and Wales (1999 figures);
97 people in Spain (2000 figures);
40 people in Switzerland (2000 figures);
3,589 people in Mexico (2000 figures);
10,828 people in the United States (1999 figures).

The gun murder rates per 100,000 people provide a clearer picture of the international comparisons:

Canada—.54 (1999 figures);
Colombia—51.77 (2000 figures);
England and Wales—.12 (1999 figures);
Spain—.25 (2000 figures);
Switzerland—.56 (2000 figures);
Mexico—3.66 (2000 figures);
United States—3.72 (1999 figures).

Even with the recent decline in gun deaths, the number of Americans killed by guns still outpaces that of citizens in many other countries. For example, although the United States has roughly thirty-five times as many people as Switzerland, it has almost 275 times the number of gun murders each year.

Comparisons between countries can be difficult to make, however. Nations don't use the same systems to record crime and some may put crimes in different categories. In general, though, it is safe to say that gun murders occur much more often in America than in Europe and a host of other nations.

International Crime Rate Table, 1999
(not including homicides)

Country	Rate of incidents per 100 residents	% of people victimized by crime	Country rank, no. of very serious crimes
Australia	58	30	2nd
Belgium	37	21	12th
Canada	42	24	6th
Denmark	37	23	14th
Eng./Wales	58	26	1st
Finland	31	19	16th
France	36	21	10th
Japan	22	15	15th
Netherlands	51	25	5th
N. Ireland	24	15	9th
Poland	42	23	8th
Portugal	27	15	13th
Scotland	43	23	7th
Spain	30	19	11th
Sweden	46	25	4th
Switzerland	24*	18	no ranking
United States	43	21	3rd

*Switzerland's incidence rates are estimated.
Source: Crime Victims Survey (ICVS) 2000
United Nations Interregional Criminal Justice Research Institute

Five of the industrialized countries listed above had more incidents of crime (not including murder) in 1999 than the United States, but some of those crimes were relatively minor. For example, in Japan, bicycle and motorcycle theft accounted for 40 percent of the crimes. The United States had the third highest rate of crimes considered to be very serious (including car thefts, sexual assaults, and armed robbery). About one-fifth of Americans were crime victims in 1999.

International Violent Death Rate Table
(Death rates are per 100,000)

Country	Year	Total rate of murders	Total no. of murders	Total rate of gun murders
Australia[8]	2000	1.57	302	.31
Belgium	1990	1.41	n/a	.60
Canada[8]	1999	1.59	489	.54
Colombia[7,8]	2000	62.74	26,539	51.77
Costa Rica[7,8]	2000	6.57	245	3.38 (1999)
Denmark[8]	2000	1.09	58	.26
Eng./Wales[6,8]	2000	1.61	850	.12 (1999)
Finland[1,8]	2000	2.86	148	.43 (1998)
France	1994	1.12	n/a	.44
Germany[4]	2000	1.17	960	.47
Italy[8]	2000	1.01 (1999)	38	.32
Japan[8]	2000	.50	637	.02 (1994)
Mexico[7,8]	2000	14.11	13,829	3.66
Netherlands	1994	1.11	n/a	.36
Norway	1993	0.97	n/a	.30
Poland[7,8]	2000	2.47	2,170	.43
Portugal[8]	2000	2.47	247	.84
Scotland	1994	2.24	n/a	0.19
South Africa[8]	2000	51.39	21,995	23.97[9]
Spain[8]	2000	1.25	494	.25
Sweden	1993	1.30	n/a	.18
Switzerland[2,8]	2000	.96	69	.56
Thailand[7,8]	2000	n/a	n/a	33.00
Uruguay[7,8]	2000	4.61	154	2.52
United States[3]	1999	5.70	15,533	3.72
Zambia[8]	2000	7.89	797	2.31[9]

Notes:
1. The United Nations International Study on Firearm Regulation reports Finland's gun ownership rate at 50 percent of households.
2. Percentage of households with guns includes all army personnel.
3. Total homicide rate and firearm homicide rates are for 1999, FBI Uniform Crime Report (1999).
4. Percentage of households with guns excludes East Germany.
5. Number of homicides: Ministry of Interior, National Police Administration, Taiwan. Gun Homicides: Central News Agency, Taipei, November 23, 1997.
6. Total homicides and gun homicides for 1997: Criminal Statistics, England and Wales, 1997.
7. Suicide figures from World Health Organization.
8. Firearm homicide and homicide figures from Seventh United Nations Survey of Crime Trends, 1998–2000.
9. Number prosecuted.

Total no. of gun murders	Total suicide rate	Suicide by firearm rate	% households with firearms
59	12.65	2.35	19.4
n/a	19.04	2.56	16.6
165	13.19 (1992)	3.72 (1992)	29.1
21,898	7.00 (1994)	n/a	n/a
126 (1999)	11.8 (1995)	n/a	n/a
14	22.33 (1993)	2.25 (1993)	n/a
62	7.68 (1992)	.33 (1993)	4.7
22	27.26 (1994)	5.78	23.2
n/a	20.79	5.14	22.6
384	15.64	1.17 (1994)	8.9
12	2.25	1.11	16.0
n/a	16.72 (1994)	.04 (1994)	n/a
3,589	6.4 (1995)	n/a	n/a
n/a	10.30	0.31	1.9
n/a	13.64	3.95	32.0
166	30.6 (1999)	n/a	n/a
84	14.83 (1994)	1.28 (1994)	n/a
n/a	12.16	0.33	4.7
10,258[9]	n/a	n/a	n/a
97	7.77 (1993)	0.43 (1993)	13.1
n/a	15.75	2.09	15.1
40	21.28 (1994)	5.61 (1994)	27.2
20,032	8.00 (1994)	n/a	n/a
84	20.8 (1990)	n/a	n/a
10,828	12.06	7.35	39.0
233[9]	n/a	n/a	n/a

Sources:
The first seven columns of data are from the *International Journal of Epidemiology* (1998) unless noted otherwise. Column "% Households With Firearms": *Can Med Assoc J*, Killias, M (1993), except United States (Gallup [2000] and Harris [2001] polls.)

Compiled by GunCite <http://www.guncite.com>

When compared to other industrial countries, the United States scores fairly near the top when figuring homicides in general and murders by gun. The American murder rate is higher than that of nineteen of the twenty-six nations listed, including all of Western Europe. Of the countries listed, the U.S. gun murder rate is topped only by Thailand, South Africa, and Colombia. While more Americans shoot themselves to death than in other areas, the overall U.S. suicide rate is lower than in fifteen of the countries listed. Of the countries reporting the number of guns in the household, the United States is at the top of the list. Several other countries with a high number of guns per household (Canada, Finland, and Norway) have a fairly low rate of gun murders. The type of gun used (rifle, shotgun, handgun) was not reported.

According to a recent United Nations survey, Canada, England, Germany, France, Japan, the Scandinavian countries, Poland, and Spain are among the many countries with rates much lower than the United States. Mexico, Zambia, Costa Rica, and Uruguay have rates similar to those in the United States, while troubled areas such as South Africa, Thailand, and Colombia have rates far greater.

Compared with many other countries, America also has a high rate of gun-related suicides. In fact, more Americans kill themselves with guns each year than are killed by the guns of others. But when suicides from all causes are compared, the United States scores somewhere in the middle among nations of the world. For example, Americans are much more likely to shoot themselves to death than are Japanese citizens. But Japan's overall suicide rate is higher than that of the United States (16.7 per 100,000 people in Japan as opposed to 11.9 per 100,000 in the United States, in 1997).

With guns causing so many deaths and injuries, Americans agree that something needs to be done to stop the violence. They disagree—often passionately—on exactly what to do and how to do it. Deeply concerned people have approached the issue in several ways. They have called for educational programs, crime-control measures, tougher enforcement of laws, safety standards for firearms, gun-control laws, and lawsuits against gun makers. Many of the measures have met with opposition, but the most controversial has been the effort to pass laws regulating the private ownership of guns.

Arguments for Gun Control

The gun-control debate revolves around three concepts.

1) The right to bear arms mentioned in the Second Amendment. Does the Constitution guarantee the

16

right of an individual to own a gun? And if it does, can the government place any restrictions on that right?

2) The relationship between the private ownership of guns and gun violence. Does a large number of guns in the hands of armed citizens result in high rates of gun deaths and injuries?

3) The effectiveness of gun-control regulations. Do gun laws reduce the number of guns and gun deaths and injuries?

Gun-control advocates say that the more guns people have, the more deaths will be caused by them. They cite studies by private and government agencies to support this claim. For example, the FBI's Uniform Crime Reports for 1995 revealed that as more and more criminals used guns instead of other weapons, the number of deaths and injuries that occurred during robberies, burglaries, and other crimes also went up. According to a report issued by the federal Bureau of Alcohol, Tobacco and Firearms (ATF), the highest rate of violent crime and the most gun murders occurred in the early 1990s, at a time when the sales of small firearms were at a peak.

The reverse is also true, say gun-control advocates. When there are fewer guns around, the number of gun-related deaths go down. Researcher Mark Duggan reached that conclusion when he compared the number of people who owned guns with the rate of gun murders in the area. One reason gun-related deaths fall when fewer guns are available, he concluded, was because criminals can obtain guns more easily— either by stealing them or buying them secondhand—in areas where more guns exist. In places where citizens do not own guns, criminals will have a harder time obtaining them.

Armed criminals are just part of the problem, control advocates say. Instead of keeping family members safe, having a gun in the house endangers them. Accidental shootings and gun-related suicides kill more than one and one-half times the number of people killed by armed criminals. In his research, medical school professor Arthur Kellermann found that people were nearly three times more likely to be killed in homes with guns than in those without guns. A further study by Kellermann in the late 1990s showed that for every instance of a gun being used in self-defense, there were four accidental shootings, seven assaults or murders, and eleven attempted or completed suicides.

One such accidental death occurred in Jacksonville, Florida, in April 2002. Four-year-old Sabarius Mortin died after being struck in the chest by a bullet from his grandfather's gun. Apparently the boy took the handgun from a footlocker and was playing with it when it accidentally fired.

Gun-control advocates want to reduce these deaths by limiting the number of handguns in homes and by requiring locks and other safety features on guns to prevent accidental shootings.

Injuries and deaths caused by guns also have a significant effect on the American economy. According to a study by Duke University economics professor Philip J. Cook and others, gun violence costs Americans $100 billion a year in medical fees, lost wages, and other costs. That figure is divided between murders ($80 billion) and suicides ($20 billion).

Arguments for Gun Rights

Those who oppose gun-control measures give a variety of reasons for their stand. The major argument, though, is this: guns protect citizens from both criminals and a tyrannical government.

The Constitution guarantees the right to bear arms for

good reason, gun-rights supporters say. "It is the right we turn to when all else fails," then-NRA spokesman Charlton Heston said in a 1997 speech to the National Press Club. "Now, I doubt any of you would prefer a rolled up newspaper as a weapon against a dictator or a criminal intruder." Law-abiding citizens who are armed help reduce the crime rate, Heston and his supporters say. To support their argument, they cite research done by criminology professor Gary Kleck. Based on a national telephone survey, Kleck reported in 1993 that Americans used guns to defend themselves and their property 2.5 million times a year. Such use or threatened use of firearms, according to the Kleck study, saved lives, reduced injuries, and prevented theft of property.

That is what Amalio Santos did when he shot and killed a man who had broken into his home in Queens, New York, in February 2003. The music-store owner told police he found two men in his basement. The intruders ran across the lawn, Santos said, then turned and aimed a gun at him. Santos fired, hitting one man in the face. The homeowner had a permit for the gun and was not charged in the shooting.

Gun-rights advocates argue that laws aimed at controlling guns don't have the desired effect. Instead of keeping guns out of the hands of criminals, they say, such laws make it harder for honest people to protect themselves.

Furthermore, they say, eliminating guns from the home will not prevent suicides. People commit suicide by many different means and will turn to something else if guns are unavailable.

Finally, they note that firearms have always been a part of American culture. Learning to shoot and hunt is an important rite of passage in many families. Such activities, they believe, teach youngsters how to handle guns properly. Voluntary safety programs, not restrictions, are the way to prevent accidental shootings, according to gun-rights proponents.

Armed citizens who prevent crime help the U.S. economy, gun-rights advocates say. Using Kleck's figures, the

For Gun Control?— Jimi's Dilemma

Jimi (not his real name) is a young African American who has worked for gun control since he was a teenager. Jimi grew up in a lower-middle-class neighborhood in a major city. As a teenager he hung out with friends who were members of gangs, though he says he never joined one himself.

Jimi has firsthand experience with the harm caused by guns. He has witnessed shootings outside his high school and in his neighborhood. Not long ago he saw a group of men in a Cadillac shoot a man walking down his street. The man died on the spot. Jimi was playing basketball in front of his house when the killing occurred. In just one month, Jimi has heard gunshots fired into the air in his neighborhood fifteen times.

"I believe gun violence is wrong. I believe in [the gun-control] mission that we need to bring gun violence to a stop," he said. For the past three years he has worked to curb gun violence and put limits on guns. He has discussed the dangers of guns with children, encouraging them to stay away from firearms. He has even written a song urging young people not to use guns.

And yet . . .

Two people Jimi knows are involved in a deadly feud. When Jimi tried to warn one of the danger, the other threatened to kill Jimi. After that, someone shot a gun outside his door. It took police twenty minutes to respond to Jimi's call.

Frightened for his life, Jimi asked a friend to buy him a gun. Not yet twenty-one, Jimi cannot legally buy a handgun in his state. "I made a phone call and got a gun within thirty minutes," Jimi said. His friend had no trouble buying the gun at a local gun show, where there are no requirements to check the background of the buyer. The gun, an inexpensive 380-mm handgun, is known as a Saturday night special because it is so frequently used in crimes presumably most often committed on Saturday nights.

Jimi knows that getting the gun to protect himself clashes with his continuing work for gun control. "I know it's stupid, and I know it doesn't solve anything," he said of owning a gun. But, he added, he acted "according to the street code, in case someone shoots at me. It's kill or be killed."

National Center for Policy Analysis, a private research institute, estimates the actions of armed citizens save the country between $90 million and $38.8 billion a year by preventing crimes. Firearms manufacturers also say that their industry helps the American economy rather than hurting it. The industry, they say, boosts taxes collected by local, state, and federal governments, creates jobs, and generates more than $20 billion of economic activity a year.

A Complex Issue

People on both sides of the gun-control debate agree that there are many factors that lead to crime and violence. Poverty, drugs, racial discrimination, a lack of good role models, a culture focused on possessions, inadequate education and health care, the prevalence of violence on TV and in movies, video games, and music lyrics—all have been named as causes of the violent behavior too often seen in American society. Those who favor gun control argue that violence increases when guns are available. Limiting guns, they say, will reduce the number of deaths and injuries.

Those who argue against gun control believe armed citizens can help control crime and prevent killings. Gun-rights and gun-control advocates support their views with opposing interpretations of the U.S. Constitution. Both sides cite facts and figures to strengthen their case. Both claim that data used by opponents have been misinterpreted or are wildly exaggerated or both. An independent observer faces a daunting task in determining which figures to believe.

The difficulty in sorting through the data can be seen in statistics on the use of guns for self-defense. Gun-control advocates cite U.S. Department of Justice figures that

For Gun Rights?— Sue Gay's Hero

Tony Murry held a box cutter to Sue Gay's throat in the kitchen of her South Bend, Indiana, home. The man, an acquaintance of Mrs. Gay's daughter, had been convicted of theft and unarmed robbery in the past and had served time in jail. Murry was drunk when he stopped by the Gay house to visit. After Mrs. Gay asked him to leave, Murry became violent.

Struggling against her attacker, Mrs. Gay managed to shout to her grandson to call 911. Instead, the boy, eleven, grabbed a .45 and shot Murry in the chest. The man died later at a local hospital.

"One shot and he got him. He's my little hero," said Mrs. Gay, recalling how her grandson took aim and fired even though Murry had pulled Mrs. Gay in front of himself for protection. She said she thought she would be killed by the bullet, too. But she escaped unharmed. Her grandson had learned about guns when his father took him target shooting.

The fact that she had a gun in the house and that her grandson knew how to shoot saved her life, Mrs. Gay said. No charges were filed in the shooting, which police said was justifiable. "The young man reasonably believed his [grand]mother and [he] himself to be in danger of dying," said an officer investigating the incident. "He did what he had to do."

And yet . . .

Police said the fact that guns were in the house may have been what led Murry to the Gay residence in the first place. Gay's late husband had collected guns. Murry, who had been to the house before, knew that the Gays had guns on the premises. "He told me, 'Take me to where the guns are,'" Mrs. Gay told reporters.

show victims of crime use firearms to defend themselves and their property about 100,000 times a year. Gun-rights advocates cite the Kleck telephone survey, which puts the figure at 2.5 million. A study for the National Institute of Justice estimates Americans use guns in self-defense about 1.5 million times a year.

Gun control fuels the passions of millions of Americans on both sides of the argument. It is a very complex issue, and the efforts to control the use and ownership of guns by private citizens have sparked intense controversy and debate.

2
The Second Amendment

A well regulated Militia, being necessary to the security of a free State, the right of the people to keep and bear Arms, shall not be infringed.

This is the text of the Second Amendment to the U.S. Constitution. It is part of the Bill of Rights, which guarantees a number of specific freedoms to individual citizens. The Second Amendment lies at the heart of the gun-control debate. The argument centers on the meaning of the amendment and whether it supports an individual person's right to own a firearm or only the right of states to maintain an independent militia.

Articles of Confederation

Volunteer militiamen fought alongside the regular army during the American Revolution. When the nation's founders

wrote the Articles of Confederation, they included militias in
the document.

Written in 1777 and adopted in 1781, the articles served
as a guide for the new nation during its struggle for independence. The articles established a central Congress, made
up of representatives of each state, which would direct the
new nation's business. Although the individual states kept
their independence, the Articles of Confederation barred
them from having their own armies during peacetime without permission from Congress. To offset the power granted
the central government, however, the articles required each
state to "always keep up a well regulated and disciplined
militia, sufficiently armed and accoutered [equipped]." Arms
and ammunition for the militia were to be stockpiled by
each state and distributed when needed, in times of unrest or
other emergencies. The document does not mention a separate right of individual citizens to bear arms.

States also created charters, several of which spelled
out the right of citizens to own guns. Most of these clauses
linked the right to bear arms to protection of the state and
society as a whole. For example, Virginia's constitution,
adopted in 1776, said "that a well regulated militia, com-
posed of the body of the people, trained to arms, is the
proper, natural, and safe defense of a free state." Likewise,
Tennessee's constitution, adopted in 1796, guaranteed
that "freemen of this State have a right to keep and bear
arms for their common defence." In some cases, states
added that citizens had a right to protect *themselves* as
well as the state with firearms. For example, Pennsylvania's constitution of 1790 stated, "The right of the citizens
to bear arms in defence of themselves and the State shall
not be questioned." Today, forty-four of the fifty states
mention the right to bear arms in their constitutions. Six
have no such clause.

The Bill of Rights

Once the war ended, the United States disbanded its regular army. Individual states relied on their own militias to quell riots and protect citizens from hostile Native Americans. Militia members were male citizens, armed with their own guns, who underwent training, took part in military exercises, and served on a temporary basis when needed to protect the state and its inhabitants.

That arrangement was put to the test in 1786 when disgruntled farmers, led by Daniel Shays, rebelled against high taxes and jail terms for debtors in Massachusetts. The law required people who could not pay their bills to be put in jail. Shays' band prevented courts in several towns from hearing cases. Some members of the local militia refused orders to oppose the armed mob, which included friends and neighbors. In response, Congress voted to establish an army to fight Shays and his men as well as to suppress uprisings that were occurring in other areas. Before the federal army had time to form, the Massachusetts governor recruited several thousand men, who crushed the Shays' Rebellion in 1787.

Shays' Rebellion helped convince American leaders that the new nation could not manage effectively with the weak federal government established in the Articles of Confederation. The U.S. Constitution, drawn up by the fifty-five delegates to the Constitutional Convention in 1787, gave Congress and the federal government broad powers to raise armies and to control militias when they were needed to protect the country. But the nation's founders also recognized the dangers of turning over all power to a strong federal government.

In its original form, the Constitution did not contain a list of people's specific rights. One group of delegates, known as the Federalists, argued that such a list was not

THIS ETCHING DEPICTS AN ARMED MOB AS IT SEIZES CONTROL OF A MASSACHUSETTS COURTHOUSE DURING A REVOLT THAT BECAME KNOWN AS SHAYS' REBELLION. DANIEL SHAYS, A REVOLUTIONARY WAR VETERAN AND FARMER, LED THE REBELLION, WHICH RAGED IN MASSACHUSETTS FOR SIX MONTHS IN 1786 AND 1787. AFTERWARD, THE FEDERAL GOVERNMENT WAS GIVEN BROAD POWERS TO RAISE ARMIES AND MILITIAS TO CRUSH CITIZENS' REBELLIONS.

necessary. In their view, the new Constitution put enough limits on the federal government's powers. But the anti-Federalists disagreed. The memory of King George III's efforts to control his American subjects remained fresh in their minds. They wanted to document the rights of the individual as a safeguard against a tyrannical federal government. Anti-Federalists especially feared that the federal government—with its ability to form an army—could overpower the states and their citizens.

Thomas Jefferson argued forcefully for a separate bill of rights. The man who had drafted the Declaration of Independence and who would later serve as the nation's third president made a passionate plea for a document that would protect the rights of individual Americans: "A bill of rights is what the people are entitled to against every government on earth, general or particular, and what no just government should refuse, or rest on inference."

Support for that view threatened the adoption of the new Constitution. In the end, the states did ratify the Constitution, in 1788, but only with assurances that a bill of rights would soon follow. Several states had already included a bill of rights in their own constitutions. The one written by George Mason for Virginia served as a model for what became the nation's bill of rights. James Madison, also a Virginian, who later served as America's fourth president, prepared a draft of the bill in the form of twelve amendments to the Constitution. The final version, with ten amendments, won Congress's approval, and after ratification by three-fourths of the states, in 1791, the Bill of Rights became part of the Constitution.

The Bill of Rights guaranteed a broad range of freedoms, including speech, assembly, and religion. The Second Amendment provided for the right to keep and bear arms. It tied this right to the need for "a well regulated

KNOX TRAIL LIBRARY

militia." Both sides in the gun-control debate agree that the founders adopted the amendment to protect citizens against an all-powerful federal government, which had the right to maintain an army during peacetime as well as in war. Beyond that, the two sides have sharp differences about the meaning of the amendment and exactly what the founders had in mind when they wrote it.

Individual Rights

Gun-rights advocates believe the founders wrote the Second Amendment to help ease fears of a government takeover by allowing citizens to keep their guns. They define the term "the people" in the second clause of the amendment as meaning individual Americans. The amendment, they contend, does not refer to states' rights. This viewpoint is known as the individual-rights or personal-rights argument. Supporters of this position argue that the Constitution had already given the federal government power over state militias and forbade the states from keeping armies without Congress's approval. Therefore, they reason, the right guaranteed in the Second Amendment must refer to individuals rather than to a militia already under the control of the federal government.

In testimony before the Senate in 1998, leading gun-rights advocate Eugene Volokh likened the right of the people to bear arms to the rights stated in the First, Fourth, and Ninth Amendments. All four, he noted, refer to "the right of the people," not to states' rights. "These rights are clearly individual," Volokh, a professor at the University of California at Los Angeles Law School, told the senators. "They protect 'the right of the people' by protecting the right of each person."

According to this line of thought, armed citizens offer

protection to the community as a whole. A tyrannical federal government might have second thoughts about trying to oppress citizens who are armed and prepared to fight. These individual, able-bodied, armed citizens, Volokh said, make up the "well regulated militia" referred to in the first clause of the Second Amendment. Noting that today's courts require equality of the sexes, Volokh testified, "I feel comfortable saying that every able-bodied citizen from age seventeen to forty-five, male or female, is a member of the militia."

Akhil Reed Amar, a Yale University law professor and Bill of Rights expert, believes the authors of the Second Amendment had the American patriots in mind when they wrote the provision. According to Amar, the amendment grants small groups of people the right to defend their homes. "They weren't thinking of establishing a right for the National Guard or for the Michigan militia [a private armed group linked to Timothy McVeigh, the Oklahoma City bomber]," Amar said. "They were thinking about Lexington and Concord, where they stood with their families and friends to resist an imperial army."

Collective Rights

People advocating increased control of gun ownership view the Second Amendment in very different terms. They see the amendment as guaranteeing states' rights to form militias to protect against a strong federal army. The amendment does not, they contend, guarantee the right of individual citizens to own and carry firearms. When the framers referred to "the people" in the amendment, according to this viewpoint, they meant the citizens as a group. This is called the collective-rights argument.

Those who support the collective-rights argument focus

on the importance of the first clause of the Second Amendment. The "well regulated militia," they contend, refers to the collection of men who served as part-time soldiers when called upon in an emergency. This militia, they argue, did not include the entire population but was limited to able-bodied men between the ages of eighteen and forty-five. Women, children, and older men did not participate as militia members.

These gun-control advocates argue that the Second Amendment was written to protect the right of those citizens who were members of the militia to own guns needed for military purposes. The framers of the Bill of Rights, in other words, guaranteed that the people had an armed militia ready to defend them against a tyrannical federal government. Therefore, they argue, it is perfectly acceptable to pass laws to control guns owned by private individuals who are not connected with the military. According to gun-control advocates, the militia to which the Second Amendment refers no longer exists. In the more than 200 years since the Bill of Rights was written, the military has changed dramatically. Today, they say, the National Guard serves as the state's "militia." Within that "well regulated" organization, citizens receive training in protecting their fellow citizens. The fringe militias run by private citizens are not at all like the militias mentioned in the Bill of Rights. To put the defense of the citizenry in the hands of these unregulated, armed bands, they say, would be dangerous as well as ineffective.

Furthermore, proponents of gun control argue, the framers of the U.S. Constitution established a government ruled by the people. The safeguards built into the Constitution itself assured that the people could change an unpopular government or even overthrow it by peaceful means without having to resort to gunfire.

3
The Role of Guns in America's History

European colonists who settled in America brought guns with them to kill game for food and to protect against the native peoples already living in the New World. Settlers relied on guns as one of the tools for survival in the American wilderness. Even so, gun ownership was hardly universal among the new Americans. Among the English adventurers who settled Jamestown, Virginia, in 1607, only the well-to-do men owned firearms.

The settlers quickly learned the value of having a force of armed men to protect their new colonies against hostile Indians and other enemies. In 1631 Massachusetts Bay passed laws that required all able-bodied men in the colony to join the militia. Militia members were expected to supply their own guns. Other settlements passed similar laws, some requiring that all able-bodied men own a firearm. However, many men—even those in the militia—could not afford a gun or did not have one that fired properly.

When King George III ordered troops to America to restore order in 1768, militias of defiant colonists resisted the British soldiers. On April 19, 1775, the militia known as the Minutemen stood their ground in Lexington and Concord, Massachusetts. But it soon became apparent that the Americans could not rely on militias alone to defend against the disciplined, well-armed British troops. The newly formed Congress established the Continental Army, headed by George Washington, to lead the resistance. Congress also voted to buy weapons and ammunition for the army. The guns, bought mostly from France and Holland, helped fill the need for weapons. Still, one-quarter of the U.S. forces did not have guns in the summer of 1776.

Colt's Revolutionary Gun

In 1836 Sam Colt invented a revolver that changed the firearms industry forever. Colt's new gun enabled shooters to fire up to six times in rapid succession without stopping to reload. The revolver was not only more efficient than other guns but also less expensive. A saying attributed to western gun lovers of the time showed the impact of Colt's invention: "God created men; Colonel Colt made them equal." Using state-of-the-art machinery and assembly lines, American factories soon led the world in the production of firearms.

Gun ownership in the United States, and the popular image of the gun-packing American, got a boost in the middle of the nineteenth century. When a miner discovered gold in a ditch at a California sawmill in 1849, a wave of adventurers and gold seekers rushed west. Congress passed a special law allowing the U.S. government to sell guns to these new pioneers. As the area became more settled and cities formed their own police forces,

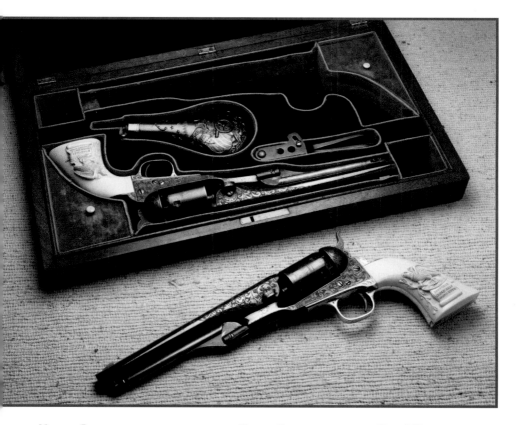

HENRY SHERIDAN, A GENERAL IN THE UNION ARMY DURING THE CIVIL WAR,
OWNED THIS SET OF COLT REVOLVERS. SAM COLT'S REVOLVER, INTRODUCED
IN THE LATE 1830S, WAS MORE EFFICIENT AND LESS EXPENSIVE THAN OTHER
MODELS OF THE TIME. IT BECAME POPULAR WITH GUN BUYERS ALL OVER
AMERICA, ESPECIALLY THOSE IN THE WEST.

many found they did not need firearms. Books and movies about frontier life, however, made it seem as if the West was filled with gun-toting cowboys and marshals who tried to control them with their own six-shooters.

But it was war, not gold, that really determined the gun's future prevalence in American life. The Civil War in the 1860s greatly increased the number of firearms in America, as armies of both the North and the South quickly added to their supply with guns from abroad. The war also increased the guns' deadliness. At the beginning of the conflict, soldiers mostly used rifles capable of firing only one shot before being reloaded. But as the war wore on, new American models such as Springfield and Enfield rifles allowed soldiers to fire repeatedly without reloading. These guns were a big improvement over the muskets used in previous wars.

Taking Guns Home

At war's end, the government allowed Union soldiers to keep the guns they had used on the battlefield. Most Confederate soldiers had to turn in their rifles and other long guns, but many kept their pistols. Ulysses S. Grant, who had commanded the Union forces, allowed Confederate officers to keep their side arms because he did not want to humiliate them. The effect of these decisions was dramatic. Armed soldiers returning to their homes changed the nation from one in which private citizens owned a few hundred thousand guns to one in which more than a million guns were in private hands.

Following the Civil War, the nation endured a period of great unrest as freed slaves and defeated whites struggled to find their place in the new South. During Reconstruction, federal troops intervened many times to stop armed mobs of white men from killing Southern blacks. Armed Ku Klux Klan members and other white-supremacist groups carried out raids against black citizens well into the twentieth century. In a few instances, groups of armed black men, many of whom had fought with Union troops during the Civil War, went on the attack, but they were soon overpowered by better-armed and more-organized white militias. During the same period, crime and economic unrest plagued Northern cities. Police saw a sharp rise in the use of handguns for crime. The number of people who used guns to commit suicide also increased.

Founding the National Rifle Association

With the military no longer buying guns after the Civil War, firearms manufacturers began mass-producing cheap handguns for civilians and rifles for hunters. They also developed markets overseas. More people became interested in shooting as a sport. In 1871 Colonel William C. Church and General George Wingate, who had served as Union officers, formed the National Rifle Association. Disturbed by the poor marksmanship of troops under their command during the war, they formed the group to "promote and encourage rifle shooting on a scientific basis."

The rifle club promoted shooting as a sport, recruiting young men at colleges and schools. By 1906 more than 200 boys competed at NRA matches at the New Jersey shooting grounds. People from many walks of life embraced the sport, from clergymen to children who won guns at local carnivals. Colleges taught courses in shooting. Few people of the time objected to gun ownership by private Americans.

Experts debate just how many people owned guns in

the late 1800s. The version of history shown in films certainly exaggerates the number of guns at the time and their use in crime. But gun ownership appears in fact to have been commonplace across the country, even in large eastern cities like New York. An article in the *New York Tribune* in 1892 noted this trend: "Let a mad dog take a turn about Times Square, and the spectator is astonished to see the number of men who will produce firearms." By the 1890s, Americans owned 750,000 pistols, 400,000 shotguns, and 500,000 rifles. Gun ownership continued to increase in the 1900s as workers' salaries rose and gun prices decreased.

Between 1899 and 1945 Americans bought more than 44 million guns, including almost 11 million handguns (pistols and revolvers).

Gun Ownership Today

Private individuals in the United States now own between 220 million and 230 million firearms. About 70 million of those weapons—roughly one-third—are handguns. Americans buy an additional 4.5 million to 5 million new guns each year. The number of guns owned by private Americans has more than doubled in the past thirty years. Nevertheless, a large majority of Americans—65 percent to 71 percent—do not own guns, according to the National Institute of Justice. Of course, that means that the rest own one or more guns each, and various polls show that between 35 percent and 41 percent of American homes have a gun in them. Gun makers in the United States produced more than 5 million guns in 1994, just as a major gun-control law was going into effect. Since then the number of handguns produced has dropped by 50 percent, while rifle sales have gone up somewhat.

4
Early Gun Laws

The Bill of Rights gives citizens specific rights that cannot be taken away. However, that does not mean that no limits can be placed on those rights. The First Amendment guarantees free speech for all citizens, but it is still against the law for a citizen to lie under oath or to shout "fire" in a crowd with the intention of causing a riot. Likewise, Congress can attach limits to other freedoms listed in the Bill of Rights, including the right to bear arms.

Several states have included in their constitutions a specific right of state government to regulate gun ownership. Florida's constitution, for example, states, "The right of the people to keep and bear arms in defense of themselves and of the lawful authority of the state shall not be infringed, except that the manner of bearing arms may be regulated by law." Georgia and Texas use similar words in their constitutions granting state government the authority to rule on the bearing of arms. Colorado's constitution contains a clause that focuses specifically on concealed firearms, noting that nothing in that document "shall be construed to justify the practice of carrying concealed weapons."

Regardless of which interpretation of the Second Amendment one supports, almost everyone agrees that some limits are needed to keep order. State and federal laws bar criminals from owning guns. Other laws stop children from having or using firearms. People are not allowed to shoot guns near homes or other populated areas.

The late Supreme Court Chief Justice Warren Burger, a gun owner himself, supported the view that the government has the right to place limits on gun ownership. The Second Amendment does not guarantee every citizen the right to own "any kind of weapon," Burger said, in a 1991 television interview. "Surely the Second Amendment does not remotely guarantee every person the constitutional right to have a Saturday night special or a machine gun without any regulation whatever. There is no support in the Constitution for the argument that federal and state governments are powerless to regulate the purchase of such firearms." Gun-rights and gun-control advocates strongly disagree over the extent to which guns and their use should be limited. At one extreme, some people oppose almost all limits on guns. Those on the opposite extreme favor severe restrictions on gun owners, gun sellers, and gun manufacturers. Many more Americans hold views that fall somewhere between these extreme views on how guns should or should not be controlled.

The two sides also disagree on the effectiveness of gun regulations already in place. An estimated 20,000 local, state, and federal gun laws currently regulate firearms in the United States. Some address criminal use of firearms; others require gun owners to register their weapons. Still others concern the manufacture, sale, and purchase of firearms.

Colonial and Early American Gun Laws

As early as the seventeenth century, colonial governments passed laws to control the sale of firearms. Many of the early laws were aimed at keeping guns out of the hands of those thought to be dangerous or undesirable by the colony's leaders. Laws in several colonies banned the sale of guns to American Indians. Many colonial leaders—fearful of slave revolts—passed laws barring slaves and free blacks from owning guns. People were so afraid of a rebellion among slaves in some areas that local laws required slave masters to take their guns to church. Some northern colonies ruled by Protestants did not allow white servants and Catholics to own firearms.

Other laws arose after dissatisfied settlers, organized into informal militias, used guns to resist the colonial authorities. As a result, several colonies strengthened their gun laws. While earlier laws had required all able-bodied men to carry firearms to protect their colonies from hostile American Indians, new laws now protected colonies—and colonial leaders—against armed mobs of colonists. For example, laws passed in Massachusetts in 1692 barred private people from carrying firearms in public.

Generally, the American colonies—and later, the states—relied on constables and professional soldiers to maintain the peace. They also trained men in the community to serve in a volunteer militia. In communities that did not have enough trained officers, order was not as certain. Sometimes bands of criminals threatened the population. When that happened, armed men in the community formed their own bands, rounded up the criminals, and beat or killed them. Sometimes these armed bands of citizens also punished other groups of people they considered undesirable, such as debtors. The community leaders eventually ended the vigilantes' rule by bringing in sheriffs and setting up courts.

NAT TURNER (1800–1831) IS THREATENED BY A SLAVE HUNTER IN THIS
ENGRAVING. IN 1831 TURNER LED FELLOW SLAVES IN A REVOLT AGAINST
THEIR WHITE OWNERS, KILLING ABOUT 50 PEOPLE. IN RESPONSE, WHITE
MOBS ATTACKED AND KILLED NEARLY 200 BLACKS. AFTER THAT, SEVERAL
SOUTHERN STATES BANNED FREE BLACKS FROM OWNING OR CARRYING GUNS.

After Nat Turner led a rebellion among fellow slaves in Virginia in 1831, several Southern states tightened their gun-control laws. Virginia repealed laws that had allowed free blacks to carry weapons under certain circumstances, thus making it illegal for free blacks "to keep or carry any firelock of any kind, any military weapon, or any powder." In 1834 Tennesseeans revised their constitution, which had guaranteed the right to keep and bear arms to "the freemen" of the state, to apply only to "free white men." An 1840 law in North Carolina required free blacks to register guns with the court.

During this time a number of states and local areas passed gun laws to protect the public safety. In the mid-1800s a New Jersey law made it illegal to carry a gun on other people's property without written permission from the landowner. A proclamation issued by the Washington, D.C., mayor's office on December 23, 1828, attacked the local custom in that city of firing gunshots to celebrate Christmas and New Year's "to the great annoyance of the peaceable inhabitants of this city, and to the manifest danger of their persons and property." The mayor declared that those who persisted in the custom would be arrested for disorderly conduct.

Black Codes

The Civil War provided guns to many people, including blacks, who had not owned them before. Following the war, Southern states, attempting to reassert control over former slaves, quickly passed laws that severely limited blacks' freedoms. Called Black Codes, and later referred to as Jim Crow laws, these discriminatory statutes barred blacks from owning guns, among other restrictions.

After the Civil War, Congress took several actions to expand the rights of African Americans. Congress overrode President

Andrew Johnson's veto to pass the Civil Rights Bill of 1866. This bill granted equal rights to all people born in the United States, including former slaves. The Reconstruction Acts, which Congress passed the following year, divided the South into sections under federal control and gave African-American men the right to vote. The Fourteenth Amendment, adopted in 1868, further strengthened the rights of African Americans. The amendment made it illegal for states to "make or enforce any law which shall abridge the privileges or immunities of citizens" and said that states must grant "to any person within its jurisdiction the equal protection of the laws." This amendment enabled the federal government to take action against the states to protect the rights of individual citizens.

Despite these advances, African Americans would not have true equality for another century. A steep drop in the economy in the 1870s ended Reconstruction. As part of a congressional compromise in 1877 that gave Rutherford B. Hayes the presidency in a fiercely disputed election, the United States withdrew the federal troops still remaining in the South. Southern states regained power and, with the help of state courts, reinstated strict gun laws that applied only to blacks and in some cases to poor whites. Meanwhile, Southern whites used guns to reinforce their power. Violence against blacks became commonplace. In 1876 Wade Hampton became governor of South Carolina with the help of gun- and rifle-club members who threatened African-American voters. According to a federal report of the time, more than 1,000 blacks died at the hands of white extremists in 1868 in Louisiana alone.

Northern Crime and Western Guns

The Civil War and the unrest that followed affected the North as well as the South. Responding to a rising crime rate, Northern cities began passing gun-control laws. In 1866

New York City made it a misdemeanor to shoot a gun in the city. Another law, passed that same year, prohibited people from carrying concealed brass knuckles and other items but did not include pistols in the list of banned weapons. A law enacted a decade later, in 1877, required people to have a permit to carry a concealed weapon, but officials seldom denied a request. In 1905, however, the city strengthened the law considerably by approving a fine of up to $250 and a maximum jail sentence of six months for violators.

Some of the Northern laws mirrored Southern legislation aimed at certain groups of people. New York State, for example, passed a law in the early 1900s banning aliens (immigrants) from carrying firearms in public.

Even in the West, some began agitating against the growing number of gun deaths. Texas led the nation in homicides in 1870. As part of a campaign to reduce the violence, two Texas cities—Galveston and Houston—made it illegal to carry concealed weapons and fined violators $100. Ranch owners joined forces with newspaper reporters in 1882 and called on cowboys to stop carrying guns. Noting that gun violence among cowboys cost the ranchers money, one reporter urged them to stop hiring "those cowboys who cannot move, eat, or sleep without being armed to the teeth like a . . . bandit." By the early 1900s, westerners had passed many laws regulating guns. A 1907 Texas law taxed sellers of revolvers 50 percent of their total earnings. During the same period, a person convicted of pointing a gun at someone in Oklahoma faced three months in jail and a $50 fine.

From State Laws to Federal Involvement

Despite rising crime, most Americans at the time did not turn to the federal government for answers. Instead, states and cities responded to public outcries by passing a hodgepodge of bills, among them laws that regulated deadly weapons. Often legislators passed these laws after a particularly gruesome or notorious crime occurred. In 1910, for example, an unhappy city worker who had been fired shot New York City Mayor William Gaynor in the throat in an unsuccessful assassination attempt. The following year novelist David Graham Phillips was gunned down on the street by a mentally ill musician.

In response, New York passed the Sullivan Law in 1911, a landmark piece of legislation that set the stiffest controls on guns in the nation and the first attempt in America to apply such restrictions to all civilians. Under the law, a person had to have a police permit to buy or possess a handgun or other weapon that could be concealed. Despite opposition from the National Rifle Association, which charged that the law would "have the effect of arming the bad man and disarming the good one," the law passed without difficulty.

A Call for National Gun Control

The Eighteenth Amendment and passage of the Volstead Act in 1920 banned the sale of liquor in the United States. Prohibition, as the ensuing thirteen-year period was called, was a colossal failure. Citizens ignored the ban on alcohol, and bootleggers flourished. Gangsters armed with machine guns bribed officials and flouted the law. Cities and states were powerless to stop the corruption. Their plight put pressure on the federal government to fight crime and control guns.

The American Bar Association (ABA) lobbied for national gun-control laws that would stop companies from making firearms except for police and military uses. "We find that the laws prohibiting the carrying of firearms or deadly weapons are ineffective—in fact, that they work to the benefit of the criminal rather than to the law-abiding citizen," noted an article in the *ABA Journal* of 1922. "The revolver serves no useful purpose in the community today."

According to a study conducted by the ABA, pistols were used in nine out of ten murders in the United States. The ABA estimated that more than 9,500 murders were committed in the United States in 1921. "The criminal situation in the United States, so far as crimes of violence are concerned," wrote the author of the report, "is worse than that in any other civilized country."

Congress paid little attention to this and other efforts to pass a national gun-control law. In 1921 Congress killed a bill submitted by Senator John K. Shields (D-Tenn.) that sought to ban the shipment of small pistols between states.

The Uniform Firearms Act

Gun control continued to be treated as a matter for the states to handle. A shooting club called the U.S. Revolver Association worked with the NRA to produce a model law on firearms that all states could adopt. The two groups hoped this would take the place of more restrictive laws, like New York's Sullivan Law. In 1927 a modified version of the groups' proposal, called the Uniform Firearms Act, was adopted by the National Conference of Commissioners on Uniform State Laws and endorsed by the ABA. Among its provisions, the act:

- **required private individuals to obtain a license to carry concealed firearms;**
- **barred those convicted of violent crimes, children under eighteen, "drunkards, and other unfit persons" from owning a gun;**
- **limited the sale of guns to licensed dealers, who were required to record the names of buyers;**
- **established a forty-eight-hour waiting period between purchase and delivery of guns;**
- **set additional penalties for criminals using guns in the commission of a crime.**

The framers of the act did not require statewide registration of handguns because they said such a requirement would be difficult to enforce. While several states already had gun registration laws (most notably New York), others had rejected them. Arkansas, they noted, had repealed its licensing law after a two-year trial period on the grounds that it could not be enforced.

States were not required to enact the legislation, which covered only pistols and revolvers. Pennsylvania adopted the entire act in 1931. New Hampshire, Connecticut, New Jersey, and Oregon were among states that adopted at least parts of the act. Several other states rejected the act for different reasons. Arizona's governor vetoed the act, saying it was too drastic and interfered with the rights of individual Americans. Taking the opposite view, Franklin D. Roosevelt, then governor of New York, vetoed the act because it would have replaced stricter state gun laws already in place.

A Barrage of Bullets

Conflicts between rival bands of gangsters became increasingly violent and more public in the 1920s. Gangsters had begun carrying tommy guns, submachine guns named after inventor John T. Thompson that had been used in World War I. Their blatant use of the weapons reached a peak on September 20, 1926, as a half-dozen cars drove slowly down Chicago's Twenty-second Street. Suddenly, in an explosion of noise and smoke, a barrage of bullets smashed through the windows and wood of the Hawthorne Hotel, a nearby restaurant, a barbershop, a deli, and a laundry. Gangster Hymie Weiss and his men unleashed more than 1,000 shots during the attack, according to police estimates. The intended target of the shooting, rival gangster Al Capone, escaped unharmed.

This shocking display of gun power on a public street, along with protests from outraged citizens, helped convince political leaders that something had to be done. In February 1927, Congress passed a bill proposed by Representative John F. Miller (R-Wash.) that made it illegal to use the U.S. mail to ship handguns across state lines. The law, which applied only to private citizens, proved virtually worthless in curbing gun sales. Those who wanted to buy a gun simply used private shipping firms to deliver the order. The law did serve one purpose, though. It marked the first time the federal government had taken action to control guns nationally. Despite this one step forward, proponents of gun control made few gains in the 1920s.

Although crime control was an issue among Americans, gun control received much less attention. Gun-rights proponents argued that individual citizens needed guns to protect themselves against criminals. Others asserted their right, under the Constitution, to bear arms. Arms manufacturers added their weight to the argument, successfully lobbying Congress to protect their business. Their combined efforts helped convince legislators in Arkansas, Michigan, and Virginia to repeal laws already on the books that required firearms registration.

The National Firearms Act of 1934

The continuing crime wave, the Depression, and the presidency of Franklin D. Roosevelt all contributed to the push for greater gun control by the federal government in the 1930s.

As governor of New York, Roosevelt had supported the restrictive Sullivan Law and had called for a ban on machine guns. After being elected president in 1932, Roosevelt greatly increased the role of the federal government.

His administration's programs, including measures to control crime, aimed to rescue a nation in the grip of the Great Depression.

Roosevelt himself had been the intended target of an assassin's bullet. In February 1933, a disgruntled bricklayer named Guiseppe Zangara shot five bullets at the president as he spoke at a rally in Miami, Florida. The bullets missed Roosevelt but hit Chicago Mayor Anton Cermak and four other people. Cermak later died of his wounds. The incident stirred up antigun sentiment among citizens once more.

The Justice Department, under the leadership of Attorney General Homer Cummings, led the effort to pass a strong federal gun-control bill. The aim of the National Firearms Act of 1934, dubbed the "anti-machine gun" act, was to prevent gangsters from getting the machine guns and other weapons they used to terrorize their enemies and ordinary citizens. The original bill also called for national registration of all handguns, but gun-rights supporters pressured Congress to omit that part of the legislation.

As Congress was considering the bill, notorious bank robber John Dillinger escaped from jail after being arrested for killing a police officer. Public alarm over the escape helped focus attention on the need for crime control. The final bill, passed by Congress in June 1934, helped cut off the supply of firearms to gangsters. Under the act's provisions, manufacturers and gun dealers had to pay a $200 tax (approximately $2,525 in today's money) on every sale of machine guns, sawed-off shotguns, silencers, and other weapons typically used by gangsters of the day. The act also required that all such firearms be registered and that buyers be fingerprinted, have their backgrounds checked, and wait several months before obtaining their weapons. The bill applied only to so-called gangster guns; it did not restrict the sale of pistols, revolvers, shotguns, and rifles.

The Federal Firearms Act of 1938

The Federal Firearms Act of 1938 put further restrictions on those selling and shipping firearms to out-of-state buyers and buyers in foreign countries. Like the previous firearms act, the new law required sellers to get a federal firearms license and record the names and addresses of all their gun buyers. But unlike the 1934 act, the 1938 version required the much lower license fee of one dollar. This allowed people who wanted to buy guns to register as dealers. They could then receive firearms without restriction. Gun dealers and manufacturers were barred from selling firearms to people who had been convicted of certain crimes or who did not have permits required by state law. However, the law did not punish sellers who unknowingly sold guns to those not allowed to own a firearm. Neither did the law require sellers to ask customers to prove their identity. It did not cover private sales of firearms.

Because of the law's weaknesses, the Justice Department opposed its passage. Nevertheless, Congress passed the bill, with the support of the National Rifle Association, in June 1938.

Though the federal firearms acts placed only limited controls on guns, they did set a precedent for federal involvement in the issue. After passage of the 1934 law, the incidents of gangsters wielding submachine guns decreased. But even though the law helped reduce sales of submachine guns, other factors played a greater role in ridding the streets of the tommy gun. Among them were the end of Prohibition in December 1933; the increased efforts of the federal government to combat crime; and the passage of state laws to stop the production and sale of submachine guns.

The legislation of the 1930s would mark the last successful federal efforts to control guns for many years to come. At the end of the decade America would trade economic woes for military ones. Congress, preoccupied with World War II and the following economic boom, would not pass another major gun-control bill until 1968.

5
The Gun Control Act of 1968

As with previous wars, World War II created a huge market for U.S. arms manufacturers. Factories increased production to meet the government's demand for weapons. At war's end, arms makers geared up to produce guns for the civilian market. Guns from foreign countries, made during the war, began pouring into the country. Shooting clubs gained popularity, and membership in the National Rifle Association soared as the organization increased efforts to recruit hunters. Presidents Harry S. Truman and Dwight D. Eisenhower praised the NRA's shooting programs for youth.

The motto over NRA headquarters proclaimed the organization's focus: "**Firearms Safety Education, Marksmanship Training, Shooting For Recreation.**" In the postwar years, the few attempts to limit guns nationally met with indifference.

By the mid-1950s the U.S. gun market was flooded

with cheap, foreign imports. Efforts to control guns focused on protecting the domestic market rather than restricting gun ownership. Senator John F. Kennedy (D-Mass.) proposed a bill in 1958 to ban imports of guns made for military use. Kennedy's home state had a number of gun manufacturers, and the bill aimed to protect their business from foreign competition. Congress rejected the bill but did pass related legislation that banned the reimporting of guns made in the United States and sent to foreign countries as part of an aid package. It was one of the few gun control bills to win Congressional approval during this time. Thirty-five gun-control bills, all opposed by gun-rights proponents, were defeated.

Government regulations adopted in 1958 required dealers to keep records for ten years, rather than the six-year period previously in effect. The new regulations also required manufacturers to put serial numbers on all guns except .22-caliber rifles. The inexpensive .22 was primarily used for informal target shooting and hunting small game. At the time, few called for tougher enforcement of federal gun laws, and the public showed little interest in gun control. The number of cheap imported guns—the so-called Saturday night specials—continued to rise dramatically during the next decade. By 1968 Americans were importing more than 1.2 million handguns and 544,000 rifles and shotguns a year.

At the same time, the rate of violent crime, on the decline since the mid-1930s, began increasing. According to FBI reports, murder rates rose from 4.6 for every 100,000 people in 1950 to 7.9 per 100,000 in 1970. In addition, more young people were involved in violent crime.

Studies conducted by the Senate Subcommittee on Juvenile Delinquency in the early 1960s showed that "criminals, immature juveniles, and other irresponsible persons" were getting guns by mail order when state and local laws barred them from buying weapons through other means. As a result of the subcommittee's report, Senator Thomas Dodd (D-Conn.) proposed an amendment to the Federal Firearms Act in the summer of 1963. The bill banned the sale of mail-order handguns to anyone under eighteen. It also tightened dealer requirements in an effort to stop the growing numbers of gun buyers who posed as dealers.

Kennedy Assassinated

On November 22, 1963, Lee Harvey Oswald shot and killed President John F. Kennedy as he rode in a motorcade through the streets of Dallas, Texas. Oswald used a lightweight Italian rifle with a telescopic sight. He got it through mail order for $19.95.

For three days Americans watched the gruesome images of gunshots ripping through their president's body play over and over again on national television. They watched horrified as Jack Ruby shot Oswald while the television cameras rolled. Responding to the national tragedy and rising calls for gun control, Senator Dodd added a measure to his bill to regulate shotguns and rifles as well as handguns. Others in Congress introduced a total of seventeen bills on gun control, and state legislators addressed the issue in more than 170 bills.

At hearings on the gun-control bills, opponents lobbied hard against what they viewed as an infringement of their rights. Those who supported the bills argued equally passionately for laws they believed were necessary to protect the nation and individual citizens.

In 1964 the Senate Commerce Committee voted against sending Dodd's bill to the full Senate. Other gun-control bills met a similar fate. The federal government itself stood on both sides of the issue. Although President

LEE HARVEY OSWALD HOLDS A MANNLICHER-CARCANO RIFLE AND A
NEWSPAPER. OSWALD'S WIFE, MARINA, SAID SHE TOOK THE PHOTO
AROUND MARCH 31, 1963, IN THE BACKYARD OF THEIR DALLAS HOME.
CONSIDERED ONE OF THE "BACKYARD PHOTOS" FOUND BY DALLAS POLICE,
IT SHOWS THE KIND OF RIFLE USED TO ASSASSINATE PRESIDENT JOHN F.
KENNEDY. OUTRAGE OVER THE MURDER HELPED PRESIDENT LYNDON B.
JOHNSON WIN PASSAGE OF THE GUN CONTROL ACT OF 1968.

Lyndon B. Johnson supported the gun-control effort, the U.S. Army provided surplus firearms to citizens at discount prices, and many military officers supported the anti-control stance taken by backers of gun rights.

More Shootings

The nation's attention soon shifted to the widening war in Vietnam and the increasingly violent antiwar and civil-rights movements. Johnson, determined to curb gun violence at home, asked Congress in 1965 to expand the federal role in gun control. The president's bill and a new one proposed by Senator Dodd raised gun dealers' fees; barred the sale of handguns, rifles, and shotguns to anyone under twenty-one; and banned firearms sales to out-of-state buyers. During testimony on the bills in May 1965, Senator Robert F. Kennedy (D-N.Y.), the brother of the assassinated president, spoke in favor of gun control before the Subcommittee to Investigate Juvenile Delinquency. "The great majority of these deaths [of Americans killed by guns each year]," Kennedy asserted, "would not have occurred if firearms had not been readily available. For the evidence is clear that the availability of firearms is itself a major factor in these deaths."

Although NRA officials had initially endorsed the Dodd bill, many of the group's members opposed its provisions. The board later reversed its position. When Robert Kennedy blasted the NRA for not supporting reasonable gun-control measures, NRA executive vice president Franklin Orth defended the organization's record on gun control. "The National Rifle Association," he wrote in the NRA's magazine, *The American Rifleman*, "has been in support of workable, enforceable gun control legislation since its very inception in 1871."

On June 5, 1968, a Jordanian immigrant using a cheap pistol gunned down Robert Kennedy as he campaigned for the presidency in Los Angeles. Several other tragic events involving guns occurred during that time. A six-day race riot in the Watts neighborhood of Los Angeles in August 1965 killed thirty-five people. In April 1968 James Earl Ray murdered the Reverend Martin Luther King Jr., the nation's most prominent civil-rights leader.

These events affected those involved in the gun-control campaign in different ways. While many Americans reacted to the tragedies by calling for tougher gun laws, those who supported gun rights argued that law-abiding citizens needed guns to protect themselves against such atrocities.

The day Robert Kennedy died, June 6, 1968, Congress gave final approval to the Omnibus Crime Control Act of 1968. The act included a version of Johnson's original bill to control gun sales. The new law made it illegal to ship handguns to private citizens from one state to another through the mail or by any other means. It also banned the sale of handguns to people from outside the state. But it did not cover rifles and shotguns, which Johnson had included in his bill.

Not satisfied with the new law, the president pushed for stronger regulations that would include all types of firearms. A coalition of gun-control supporters headed by astronaut John Glenn, called the Emergency Committee for Gun Control, formed to lobby for the president's proposals and stricter gun laws. They squared off against proponents of gun rights.

The President and the Gun Control Act of 1968

President Johnson made an earnest pitch for gun registration and licensing during a televised speech on June 24, 1968.

Noting that Americans licensed cars, boats, and dogs, Johnson urged Congress "in the name of sanity . . . in the name of safety and in the name of an aroused nation to give America the gun-control law it needs."

Johnson's proposals ignited the anticontrol efforts of gun-rights advocates, including an increasingly active group of NRA members. Under intense lobbying from opponents of the bill, Congress dropped several key measures. Two of those eliminated would have required all guns to be registered and all gun owners to be licensed. Senate Majority Leader Mike Mansfield told reporters he had never received so much mail on any other issue in his twenty-six years in Congress. Most of the letters opposed the gun-control bill.

To address the nation's growing violence, President Johnson also formed the National Commission on the Causes and Prevention of Violence in June 1968. In December 1969, the bipartisan commission released its report. After studying the issue extensively, the commission concluded that the large numbers of firearms available in America contributed to the nation's escalating violence. A ban on handguns and restrictions on other firearms, the commission wrote, would reduce the number of gun-related crimes and injuries. Noting that "firearms generally facilitate, rather than cause, violence," the commission recommended the "restrictive licensing of the handgun." The report described the nation's private ownership of 90 million firearms in the late 1960s as a "domestic arms buildup."

Before the commission's report was issued, Congress passed a compromise bill, the Gun Control Act of 1968, in October of that year. Though a weaker version than Johnson's original bill, the act made history as the first major gun-control law passed since 1938. One of its main goals was to keep firearms out of the hands of criminals. It made no mention of gun registration or licensing of owners.

In ushering the bill through the Senate, Senator Edward V. Long (D-Mo.) noted: "Every citizen could possess a gun until the commission of his first felony. Upon his conviction, however, [the law] would deny every assassin, murderer, thief and burglar of the right to possess a firearm in the future except where he has been pardoned . . . and had been expressly authorized by his pardon to possess a firearm."

The law focused on limiting gun shipments between states and restricting gun imports. It aimed to stop the flow of guns from states like Florida with lax gun laws to states like New York with strict firearms regulations. The law's provisions also put more pressure on dealers to make certain their customers could buy guns legally.

The act made it illegal to ship guns to out-of-state buyers. People could not legally buy a gun from a dealer or gun shop outside their state. Dealers, who were required to obtain a federal license, could legally ship guns to other states, but only to other dealers, not to private buyers. The law also required dealers to get proper identification from customers and to record all firearms sales. Under the law, dealers had to pay a ten-dollar license fee (increased from one dollar), have a place of business, and meet certain standards. Private individuals could sell a few guns to people who lived in the same state. Such sales did not have to be recorded, and private sellers did not have to check a buyer's identification.

Only dealers could import guns from foreign countries. Private citizens were barred from buying imported guns without a permit from the secretary of the treasury. Such a permit could be granted only under very limited circumstances. The law specifically banned the import of surplus military firearms.

The law also banned:

• the sale of firearms except shotguns and rifles to anyone less than twenty-one years old—a person had to be at least eighteen to buy a shotgun or rifle;

• firearms sales to people in states where such sales violated state laws;

• the sale or possession by private citizens of machine guns, sawed-off shotguns and rifles, and other "destructive devices";

• firearms sales to people under indictment (accused of a crime by a grand jury), those convicted of a crime punishable by more than one year in prison, drug users, those judged mentally ill, illegal aliens, anyone discharged dishonorably from the armed forces, and citizens who had renounced U.S. citizenship.

In addition, the law increased the prison term for criminals convicted of using a gun while committing a crime.

Both sides of the gun-control debate found fault with the law. Johnson and gun-control proponents criticized the law for not banning all cheap handguns (the type known as Saturday night specials). The law also did not require registration of all firearms or licensing of all gun owners, two provisions that gun-control advocates considered essential.

Gun-rights supporters described the statute as a "bad law" that unfairly deprived honest citizens of their right to own guns.

Enforcement Difficulties

From the beginning, the Gun Control Act of 1968 faced difficulties in reducing the flow of guns from state to state and to illegal buyers. Dealers were banned from selling guns to criminals and others, but dealers had no way of knowing whether buyers were telling the truth about their backgrounds. Police had difficulty tracking gun buyers who used false identification. Also, there was no central record of gun transactions. Dealers' records stayed in individual states rather than being reported to a federal agency. And since the law did not require private sales to be recorded, criminals and other illegal buyers could use that method to get a gun without leaving a trail. The law did, however, make it easier for courts to impose heavier sentences on criminals caught with illegal guns.

Loopholes in the law undermined efforts to reduce the number of handguns being sold. Citizens with a permit could legally import guns "particularly suitable for or readily adapted to sporting purposes." Congress failed to define what was meant by "suitable for . . . sporting purposes," but most people agreed that rifles and shotguns fell into the sporting category. Those guns could legally be imported into the country without much trouble. Handguns, however, were another matter. Gun-control advocates had hoped the law would exclude all handguns except target pistols. Importers argued that smaller guns were also used for sport and should be allowed under the exemption. The handgun rating system that the government eventually developed excluded from the U.S. market only very small guns and those that did not meet certain safety or construction standards.

Even with a limited ban on imported weapons, the number of cheap handguns coming into the United States from other countries dipped dramatically. However, U.S.

manufacturers could produce the same type of weapon legally. The law also allowed the import of gun parts, which could be used to make handguns in the United States. By 1973 U.S. factories were producing 1.6 million handguns a year for American civilians.

The Bureau of Alcohol, Tobacco and Firearms became the agency charged with overseeing federal gun laws. With the passage of the Gun Control Act of 1968, the federal government more than doubled its efforts to enforce firearms laws. Even so, it lacked the staff to do so effectively. Thousands of people applied for dealer licenses after the law's passage. They wanted to have a dealer's license so they could buy guns without the restrictions placed on ordinary citizens. By 1973 an estimated 160,000 dealers held licenses. This amounted to 60,000 more than in the early 1960s. Checking records and license applications from these additional dealers occupied much of the ATF agents' time. Nevertheless, they did make many more arrests for violations of gun laws. Convictions in gun cases rose from 89 in 1968 to 1,719 in 1973.

The arrests and convictions, however, amounted to a fraction of the suspected violations. Five years after the law's passage, one analyst estimated that a half-million violations of the Gun Control Act of 1968 occurred each year. The federal government did not have the time or the staff to deal with so many suspected violators. Gun ownership continued to rise. By the early 1970s Americans owned more than 100 million firearms.

The scarcity of information about gun sales also hindered agents' efforts to enforce the law. The federal government kept no central data on gun sales. Figures from individual states were not always available and often confusing. The figures on guns manufactured in the United States used to be based on taxes paid and on surveys. That changed in

1972, when manufacturers began submitting reports to the ATF. But private gun sales—estimated at about 30 percent of all sales nationwide—were not recorded at all.

Gun-control advocates had argued for years that piece-meal state regulations did not work. New York's tough gun laws limited gun ownership severely, allowing only people who proved a need to own a gun. A study of guns confiscated by the ATF in 1973 in New York City showed that only 5 percent of the firearms had been purchased in New York State. The remaining 95 percent had come from out-of-state sources. More than half had been purchased after the Gun Control Act took effect. Clearly the law had been unsuccessful in stopping guns from being carried across state lines.

Gun Violence on the Rise

The law also failed to reduce gun violence. The use of guns to commit crimes had been on the rise since the mid-1960s. The rate slowed for a few years after passage of the 1968 act, but then it continued to climb. In the United States as a whole, the rate of homicides caused by handguns rose three times faster than killings by other means in the five-year period from 1966 to 1971.

By the mid-1970s it became clear that the Gun Control Act of 1968 had not met the goals of its supporters. Gun-control advocates said the law failed because it was not tough enough, had too many loopholes, and had not been fully enforced. Gun-rights advocates argued that gun-control measures would never curb crime because they had little effect on criminals.

Throughout the 1970s members of Congress who supported gun control introduced dozens of bills to regulate firearms. Several bills proposed a ban on the "importation, manufacture, sale, purchase, transfer, receipt, or transportation of handguns" by everyone but police and licensed dealers and manufacturers. Representative Edward Koch (D-N.Y.) submitted a bill that would require all firearms to be registered. A tougher bill called for the licensing of gun owners as well as firearms registration. Bills proposed bans on Saturday night specials, guns not suitable for sporting purposes, and even toy guns. None of these efforts got far.

The New NRA

Those who opposed gun control had more success in pushing their agenda, in large part due to NRA money and organization. Until the 1970s most NRA leaders had focused on sport shooting and safety. Although the organization supported gun rights, it had also taken stands for moderate gun control. In 1972 an NRA official even testified before Congress in favor of a ban on cheap handguns.

But as efforts to control firearms multiplied, NRA members concerned about threats to gun ownership began pushing for a formal lobbying operation. At the request of Representative John Dingell (D-Mich.), who served on the NRA board, the organization in 1975 formed the Institute for Legislative Action (ILA) to lead lobbying efforts. NRA member Harlon Carter became the ILA's first head. At the annual NRA convention in Cincinnati, in May 1977, Carter and his supporters took control of the organization. Carter became president, and NRA member Neal Knox became director of the ILA. The event became known as the revolt at Cincinnati.

In forming the "New NRA," Carter and his team focused the group's energies on protecting gun ownership. Neal targeted the Gun Control Act of 1968, which he referred to as "an unparalleled abuse of Federal police powers leveled at an entire class of law abiding citizens." He vowed to lead the NRA in an all-out effort to repeal the law. "No gun law has ever deterred a criminal," Knox claimed. "They only deter the rights of innocent citizens." From then on, the NRA adopted a much stronger position and took on a more active role against gun control.

For the most part, Congress addressed the issue reluctantly. Many in Congress did not want to make an enemy of the NRA, which poured millions of dollars into election campaigns of politicians who shared the organization's views. Well-organized NRA members responded to any legislation that threatened to restrict gun ownership with letters, phone calls, and thousands of personal visits to members of Congress. Advocates of gun control were far less organized and had far less money.

In the end, Congress passed legislation backed by the NRA that exempted buyers of shotgun and rifle ammunition from the regulations of the 1968 law. Gun-rights supporters won another victory when firearms were omitted from the provisions of the Consumer Product Safety Act of 1972. Other efforts failed, however, including bills to lower the age for owning a gun from twenty-one to eighteen, as well as attempts by several House members to repeal the Gun Control Act of 1968 altogether.

Mixed Views

In part, Congress was reluctant to act because research on gun violence had not produced any clear picture of what caused it. In 1975 the National Commission on the Causes and Prevention of Violence concluded that gun ownership was linked to the violence in America's cities, and that handguns played a key role. However, another report issued that same year by researcher Douglas Murray said there was no evidence to back such claims. "Most of the writings are attempts to justify political prejudices . . . for or against restrictive handgun legislation," Murray stated. He contended that gun-control laws did not limit Americans' access to guns. He also concluded that violent crime rates remained unaffected by efforts to limit the number of guns.

The American public's views on gun issues were also mixed. Polls conducted in the mid-1970s showed Americans about evenly divided on a handgun ban. A majority (about two-thirds) favored gun registration. During this period, gun-control advocates began to band together to push for tighter gun laws. Their efforts in Massachusetts produced a law that set a one-year mandatory jail sentence for anyone convicted of carrying an unlicensed gun in public. A follow-up effort to ban handguns, however, met with defeat.

Citizens voted two to one against the proposal. Several states enacted waiting periods to allow time to check the identities of gun buyers before they received the firearms. President Gerald Ford, despite two would-be assassins' separate attempts to shoot him, strongly opposed gun registration and licenses. When asked about his views during the presidential debate with Jimmy Carter in 1976, Ford said he did not believe such laws decreased crime. "The person who wants to use a gun for an illegal purpose can get it whether it's registered or outlawed . . . and [such criminals] are the people who ought to go behind bars," Ford said. "You should not, in the process, penalize the legitimate handgun owner."

Nor did Carter, the Democratic candidate, take a strong stand for gun control. With neither candidate pushing for tough gun laws, the issue did not play a role in the election that year. Carter won the election in a close vote. During Jimmy Carter's presidency, Justice Department officials proposed legislation that would have banned certain types of handguns and required all firearms to be registered. Faced with opposition from gun-rights groups, Carter never had such a bill presented to Congress. Carter did support other efforts to regulate guns, but Congress opposed him. One of these proposals would have set up a computer system allowing the ATF to record the serial numbers of all new weapons and to keep track of sales by dealers. Reports on stolen weapons would also have been part of the system. With that in place, ATF agents would have been much better equipped to trace guns used in crimes. Gun-rights supporters argued that such a system also would have enabled ATF agents to keep tabs on honest citizens who owned guns. The system, they said, would be an out-and-out violation of their civil rights. After intense lobbying from gun-rights supporters, the House of Representatives refused to supply funding for the program.

6

The Brady Bill

Gun-rights supporters found a friend in Ronald Reagan, who succeeded Carter as president in 1981. President Reagan was a member of the NRA, a rancher, and a strong proponent of gun rights. And, like President Ford, he continued to oppose gun control even after a gun was used in an attempt on his life.

On March 30, 1981, a mentally ill young man named John Hinckley fired six shots at the president as he stood outside a Washington, D.C., hotel. One shot hit Reagan under his left arm. The bullet malfunctioned and did not explode. Reagan's wounds were serious, but he recovered. The president's press secretary, James Brady, did not fare as well. A bullet entered his brain, causing permanent damage and paralyzing him. A police officer and a Secret Service agent also suffered serious injury in the attack.

FORMER WHITE HOUSE PRESS SECRETARY JAMES BRADY SPOKE TO REPORTERS IN FRONT OF THE U.S. CAPITOL BUILDING ON NOVEMBER 30, 1998. BRADY SAID THE CHANGE FROM A FIVE-DAY WAITING PERIOD TO AN INSTANT BACKGROUND CHECK FOR THE PURCHASE OF HANDGUNS WOULD ALLOW MORE CRIMINALS TO BUY GUNS. HE AND HIS WIFE, SARAH BRADY, RIGHT, ARE LEADERS IN THE GUN-CONTROL EFFORT.

Hinckley bought the .22-caliber revolver used in the shooting at a Texas pawnshop for $29. Not long before the attempt on Reagan's life, Hinckley had been arrested for trying to smuggle a shotgun on board a plane. A resident of Colorado at the time, he lied about his address and criminal record when he bought the revolver. These facts, had they been known, would have prevented the pawnshop owner from selling him a gun legally.

The shooting revived calls for stricter gun laws on the federal level. Washington, D.C., had adopted one of the nation's strongest gun-control laws in 1976. The law prohibited civilians from buying handguns and from keeping loaded firearms in their homes. Stronger federal laws were needed, it was argued, to prevent someone like Hinckley from buying a gun elsewhere and bringing it to the district.

Reagan, however, continued his opposition to such legislation and maintained his alliance with the NRA. But in the years to come, Brady and his wife, Sarah, would become key players in the effort to control firearms.

The Firearms Owners' Protection Act

During Reagan's term of office, Congress lifted record-keeping rules for rifle ammunition, cut funds that would have paid for computers to aid ATF record-keeping, and passed a major gun-rights bill that repealed several key provisions of the Gun Control Act of 1968. Dubbed the Firearms Owners' Protection Act, the bill removed the ban on interstate traffic of rifles and shotguns as long as no state laws were violated. Another provision overrode state laws by allowing everyone but criminals and others under restrictions to carry unloaded firearms across state lines. This applied even in states that banned such action. The bill no longer required dealers to record ammunition sales, exempted pawnbrokers from certain rules, and allowed sales at gun shows. The bill barred the federal government from keeping a central database on gun sales or from setting up a system to register firearms, owners, or sales.

Congress did include a few gun-control measures in the bill: It retained most of the 1968 law's limits on handguns, prohibited machine guns, and tightened rules on importing gun parts. Under the new law, dealers were required to file a report with the secretary of the treasury when a buyer purchased more than one firearm at a time. The law also placed additional penalties on those convicted of using a firearm to commit a drug-related crime.

The Senate approved the measure by a vote of 79 to 15 in July 1985. Congress passed an amended version several months later, and Reagan signed the bill into law in July 1986.

State and Local Laws

During the years of Reagan's presidency, state and local communities passed their own legislation on both sides of the gun issue. In June 1981 Morton Grove, Illinois, became the first municipality in the United States to ban handguns. Its law required residents, with the exception of gunsmiths and licensed collectors, to give up their handguns.

Violators faced a $500 fine. Angry gun owners sued the town, but the district court ruled that Morton Grove had the right to pass the law to protect its citizens. The Supreme Court declined to hear an appeal of the ruling. At the opposite extreme, townspeople in Kennesaw, Georgia, voted to require a gun in every resident's home.

In 1982 more than 600,000 voters in California signed petitions supporting a proposal to regulate handguns and ban mail-order sales. After a fierce campaign in which gun-rights groups vastly outspent gun-control advocates, voters rejected the measure by a wide margin. Similar gun-control efforts failed in New Hampshire and Nevada. Other states, however, passed stricter gun-control laws.

In 1988 Maryland became the first state to issue an outright ban on Saturday night specials. The following year California prohibited residents from selling or importing certain types of automatic and semiautomatic guns.

Taking Aim at Gun Makers

In the early 1980s gun manufacturers came under fire when armor-piercing ammunition, originally developed for police use, began finding its way to criminals. The bullets whizzed through the bulletproof vests that were supposed to protect police from gunfire. Responding to police requests, Representative Mario Biaggi and Senator Daniel Patrick Moynihan, both New York Democrats, presented a bill in 1982 to stop the manufacture and sale of the ammunition. The bill stalled as gun-rights advocates protested that it would infringe on their right to bear arms. This stand alienated many police officers, who had been gun-rights allies in the past. They supported the new bill. In these same years, police groups were also greatly disturbed by the NRA's strong lobbying for the Firearms Owners' Protection Act. Many police officers opposed lifting the requirement for dealers to keep records and allowing mail-order gun sales. As a result, many of these police groups joined forces with gun-control supporters in their efforts to limit gun violence.

After a four-year campaign by police and gun-control groups to pass legislation against armor-piercing bullets,

Congress approved an amended version. Reagan signed it into law in August 1986. The statute banned the manufacture and importation of armor-piercing bullets used in handguns. But it allowed the bullets for hunting, target shooting, sporting purposes, and industrial use. The exceptions weakened the law and disturbed the police and others who had supported the original bill.

Another compromise bill, passed in 1988, banned firearms that were "invisible" to metal detectors used at airports and other facilities. The bill responded to concerns that terrorists could smuggle new plastic firearms through such screening points. However, as with previous bills, the act had a number of loopholes. Firearms that did not exactly fit the bill's description were allowed. The bill also exempted weapons bought before the law went into effect.

Gun-Control Groups Gather Support

Throughout the 1980s, gun-control groups gained strength. One group in particular, which got its start as the National Council to Control Handguns, rose to prominence. It was founded in 1974 by Dr. Mark Borinsky, after he was robbed at gunpoint. Four years later Nelson "Pete" Shields, a business executive whose son had been shot to death, became head of the group. The organization was renamed Handgun Control Inc. (HCI) in 1980. In 1989, Shields retired and Sarah Brady took over as chair. Sarah Brady, of course, was the wife of disabled Reagan press secretary James Brady. She had joined the battle for gun control in 1985 after her husband was shot. Her contacts, public-relations skills, and enthusiasm helped push gun control to the forefront of public consciousness and boosted membership in the organization. The group would later change its name to the Brady Campaign to Prevent Gun Violence.

For several years Congress had delayed a gun-control bill proposed by Senator Edward Kennedy (D-Mass.) and Representative Peter Rodino (D-N.J.). Their bill, adamantly opposed by gun-rights groups, called for a ban on cheap handguns and the parts used in making them. Even with intense lobbying by gun-control groups, the bill had little support in Congress. A similar bill in the House, which was introduced by Representative Edward Feighan (D-Ohio), called for a ban on silencers and small handguns and proposed a waiting period before a buyer could receive a handgun.

Typically, Democrats have supported gun-control efforts, believing that tough gun laws are one way to keep guns away from those who should not have them. Most Republicans have supported gun rights, focusing on the rights of individuals to own guns. Gun-rights groups contributed almost $4 million (93 percent of their total donations) to Republicans for use in the 2000 presidential election. Gun-control groups donated more than $460,000 (97 percent of their total donations) to Democrats for the presidential race that year. Each political party, however, has members who hold opposing views.

In 1987 gun-control advocates led by HCI proposed a less-restrictive bill as an amendment to the Gun Control Act of 1968. The Handgun Violence Prevention Act (later called the Brady Bill in honor of James Brady) proposed a waiting period and national background-check system of gun buyers. Under the bill, handgun buyers would have to wait seven days while police did a background check. People whose lives were in danger could get an exemption from police. The bill aimed to close up loopholes in the 1968 act that gave dealers no way to check a gun buyer's identity.

A Storm of Protests

Even without the restrictions of previous gun bills, the Brady Bill set off a storm of protests from gun-rights groups and a massive lobbying effort on both sides of the issue. Leading the charge against the bill, the National Rifle Association launched a multimillion-dollar campaign to defeat the measure. The contest pitted the NRA, with its 2.7 million members and $86 million annual budget, against Handgun Control Inc. The gun-control group had 1 million members and a comparatively tiny budget of $6.5 million. The bill never reached the House floor, and in September 1988 it died.

On January 17, 1989, a man with a criminal record killed five students outside their elementary school in Stockton, California, using a semiautomatic AK-47 assault rifle and a pistol. The gunman wounded another twenty-nine students and a teacher and then shot himself. The front-page stories and public outrage over the incident boosted the efforts of gun-control advocates. Under pressure, President George Bush placed a temporary ban on the import of AK-47s and similar guns. The ban remained in effect during Bush's presidency, but he opposed other control efforts.

Representative Feighan had reintroduced the Brady Bill to the House two weeks before the Stockton shooting. Senator Howard Metzenbaum (D-Ohio) followed suit, presenting it to the Senate in June. Members of both houses, besieged by worried parents and others concerned about growing gun violence, began signing on in support of the bill. The majority of police officers, who believed the bill would aid them in their efforts to identify illegal gun owners, also favored the measure. Opponents delayed the bill several times. Although the bill itself proposed fairly mild controls, opponents feared it would lead to stronger restrictions against guns.

Support from Former Presidents

By the spring of 1991 the Brady Bill had won support from former presidents Richard Nixon, Gerald Ford, and Jimmy Carter. Ronald Reagan, the president who had taken the strongest stand against gun control, finally gave his approval of the bill named for his wounded press secretary. "This bill—on a nationwide scale—can't help but stop thousands of illegal handgun purchases," he told news reporters in March 1991.

With this extra push, the House approved the bill in May 1991 by a 239 to 186 margin. *Time* magazine likened the battle over the bill to a gunfight won by the "bantamweight" HCI over the "giant" NRA. In the Senate, however, opponents led a filibuster to prevent a vote on the bill, which had been included in a larger anti-crime bill. The session ended without further action on the bill.

Congress had enacted a law that made it illegal to carry or fire a gun within 1,000 feet of a public school. The bill, known as the Gun-Free School Zones Act of 1990, won unanimous support from Congress and went into effect in January 1991. Congress modified the law in 1996 after the U.S. Supreme Court ruled the act unconstitutional in 1995. The Court's ruling, however, was based on the question of who had jurisdiction over schools, and not on the right of Congress to regulate firearms. The new version of the law, crafted to meet the Court's requirements, contained similar limits on guns near schools.

Testimony during the hearings on the new law centered on the growing number of students with guns. In 1990, according to the Centers for Disease Control (the federal agency dedicated to protecting the health and safety of Americans), one in twenty students carried a gun sometime during

any given month. That figure had grown to one in twelve by 1993.

In addition, the National Education Association estimated that 100,000 students had guns at school every day. Senator Herbert Kohl (D-Wisc.) said half of the students expelled from Milwaukee public schools had brought a gun to school. Kohl quoted a former Milwaukee school official in saying that "kids who did their fighting with their fists, and perhaps knives, are now settling their arguments with guns."

A New Version Proposed

In 1992 Congress debated the Brady Bill in what had become an annual exercise. And again the session ended without action on the bill. That year Democrat Bill Clinton took a strong stand in support of gun control during his campaign for the presidency. His election prodded Congress to reconsider the bill one more time.

Senate Majority Leader George Mitchell (D-Maine), Senator Metzenbaum, and others worked to produce a compromise bill that had a better chance of passage. Mitchell said later that the struggle to reach an agreement on the bill was "as long and tedious as any negotiation I have ever been involved in." In the fall of 1993, after five days and nights, the senators at last had a bill they believed might win approval. The new version set the waiting period at five days. That would be reduced to three days once a national background check system was in place. The bill mandated that the attorney general set up such a system by 1998.

Introducing the bill in the House on November 10, 1993, Representative Butler C. Derrick Jr. (D-S.C.) noted that the murder rate in the United States had increased while the numbers of murders committed by weapons other than handguns had gone down. "Handguns alone

have been responsible for the entire increase in the national murder rate from 1987 to 1992," he told his colleagues in the House.

Opponents saw the bill in a different light. Gun-rights advocates, including some Democrats, attacked the bill as an infringement on citizens' right to bear arms. "It is not an anti-crime bill," Representative Harold Volkmer (D-Mo.) charged. "This is an anti-gun bill." He warned that the Brady Bill was only a first step in the effort to ban guns altogether. Representative Philip Crane (R-Ill.) and others predicted that the bill would do nothing to reduce violent crime in the United States. They pointed to states with waiting periods where crime continued to rise.

Some in Congress saw the bill as unnecessary and too expensive to implement. The way to reduce violent crime, they said, was not to curb gun ownership but to punish criminals. "The answer is to take the violent criminal off the street, lock him up, and throw away the key," said Representative William McCollum (R-Fla.).

Still others opposed to the bill argued that honest citizens needed guns for self-defense and might suffer harm if they had to wait five days to get them.

Supporters of the bill countered opponents' arguments. While the bill alone would not end crime, Representative Cardiss Collins (D-Ill.) said, the legislation would give police another tool to keep guns out of the hands of criminals. A five-day waiting period, she said, should be only a minor inconvenience for legitimate gun buyers. Several proponents noted that states with waiting lists had stopped thousands of gun sales to criminals. Senator Bill Bradley (D-N.J.) said his state's background-check system, in place since the 1960s, had stopped more than 10,000 illegal gun sales. A federal check system, he said, would help control sales to criminals in states without such laws.

Passage at Last

Gallup polls conducted in 1993 showed that 88 percent of the American public favored the Brady Bill. This time both the House and the Senate approved the measure. On November 30, 1993, Congress enacted the Brady Handgun Violence Prevention Act. President Clinton quickly signed the bill into law. Seven years in the making, the Brady Bill represented a major victory for gun-control advocates over the NRA and other gun-rights groups. For the first time in more than a decade, a major national gun-control bill became law. It was also the only time in the past dozen years that Democrats controlled both the House and the Senate and the president was a Democrat.

The Brady Bill amended the 1968 Gun Control Act. It set a five-day waiting period for people wishing to obtain a handgun. This was a temporary measure designed to allow police or federal agents time to check whether gun buyers could legally own a firearm. The waiting period became effective in February 1994 and applied only to handguns. It ended in November 1998 when a national instant criminal-background-check system (NICS) began operating. The background checks are aimed at preventing criminals and people who are underage, have mental problems, or are otherwise ineligible from buying guns. The Brady Bill also raised the cost of a dealer's license from $10 a year to $200 for three years. Dealers pay $90 to renew a license, which is good for three years. New rules that also went into effect in 1998 made the Brady Bill apply to all firearms, not just handguns.

The Violent Crime Control and Law Enforcement Act of 1994

With the passage of the Brady Bill, Clinton resolved to expand the ban on assault weapons. His $30.2 billion bill—

the Violent Crime Control and Law Enforcement Act of 1994—banned nineteen military-style assault weapons, firearms that were copies of such weapons, and ammunition clips that held more than ten rounds. Ammunition clips and older models of assault weapons manufactured before 1994 were not covered in the bill.

The bill also provided funds for new prisons, additional police officers, and crime-prevention programs. It called for stiff penalties for criminals, including mandatory life terms for those convicted of three or more violent crimes. The bill also set death penalties for more than fifty federal offenses, including murders committed by terrorists. Some liberals and African Americans opposed the bill because of its provisions expanding death penalty cases.

But its primary opposition, when introduced in late fall of 1993, came from Republicans. They said the bill would cost too much to implement because it called for too much money for prevention and not enough for enforcement. Senator Orrin Hatch (R-Utah) accused Democrats of using the bill to win elections and called for even tougher penalties for criminals.

The House and the Senate proposed different versions of the bill. After months of delay, negotiators forged an agreement between the two houses. Supporters of the bill were stunned when the House then refused to bring the new version of the bill to a vote. Clinton accused the NRA of devising "a procedural trick" to defeat the bill's gun-control measures.

After an intense lobbying effort by the bill's supporters and gun-control advocates, the House passed the bill by a 235 to 195 margin on August 21, 1994. Forty-six Republicans joined Democrats in supporting the bill. Republicans played a crucial role in passing the bill in the Senate as well. In an extremely close vote, seven Republicans voted with fifty-four Democrats to win final passage for the bill on August 25. President Clinton signed the bill into law on September 13, 1994.

Clinton hailed passage of the law as a major step forward in the fight against gun violence. "Children will be safer and parents will breathe a little easier," the president declared. "Police officers will no longer be threatened by gangs and thugs with easy access to deadly assault weapons designed only for war."

In 1996 Congress added those convicted of a domestic violence misdemeanor to the list of people not allowed to own or buy a gun.

Critics saw the violent-crime law as another infringement on the right of citizens to bear arms. One gun-rights group, the Outpost of Freedom, said the regulations sounded as if they came out of Nazi Germany. Many gun-rights proponents believed Clinton's crime bill, the Brady Bill, and other gun-control measures gave the federal government dangerous power over individual states.

Some in the gun-rights camp went to extreme measures in their fight against federal gun-control measures. In a 1995 letter to members, the NRA referred to federal agents as "jack-booted government thugs" and said a proposed ban on semiautomatic weapons gave the agents "more power to take away our constitutional rights, break in our doors, seize our guns, destroy our property, and even injure or kill us." The letter became public shortly after Timothy McVeigh bombed the federal building in Oklahoma City in April 1995.

The accusations against federal agents, many of whom died in the bombing, outraged the public. Even former president George Bush, a firm believer in gun rights, objected to the abusive language. In protest, the former president resigned from the NRA.

Despite criticism from former allies, NRA officials defended their antigovernment position. Unsuccessful in stopping the passage of Clinton's bill, they and other gun-rights supporters continued their battle against gun control in court.

7

The Battle Goes to Court

The U.S. Supreme Court has dealt directly with the Second Amendment in only a few cases. Federal and state courts, however, have ruled on hundreds of cases that affect the gun-control issue. Traditionally most court rulings have upheld the collective-rights interpretation of the Second Amendment.

According to the American Bar Association, "the United States Supreme Court and lower federal courts have consistently, uniformly held that the . . . right to bear arms is related to 'a well regulated militia' and that there are no federal constitutional decisions which preclude regulation of firearms in private hands."

The Supreme Court ruled on the Second Amendment for the first time in 1876. The case, *United States* v. *Cruikshank*, involved William J. Cruikshank, one of the leaders of a white mob that slaughtered a group of black deputies in Louisiana during Reconstruction. The case against Cruikshank and his men included a charge that they had deprived the black men of their right to bear arms. In pressing the case, the government argued that the Fourteenth Amendment to the Constitution protected citizens' rights, including the right to assemble and the right to bear arms.

The Court disagreed. In a decision issued on March 27, 1876, the justices ruled that the Second Amendment barred Congress, not the states, from infringing on the right to bear arms. States, according to the opinion, had the right to make their own laws regulating their residents' behavior, including gun ownership, as long as the state laws did not interfere with citizens' rights as Americans. In addition, the Court ruled that the right to bear arms is not guaranteed by the Constitution:

The right there specified is that of "bearing arms for a lawful purpose." This is not a right granted by the Constitution. Neither is it in any manner dependent upon that instrument for its existence. The second amendment declares that it shall not be infringed; but this, as has been seen, means no more than that it shall not be infringed by Congress. This is one of the amendments that has no other effect than to restrict the powers of the national government.

The *Cruikshank* ruling has been cited in other cases to support the argument that bearing arms "is not a right granted by the Constitution."

In another early case on the Second Amendment, *Presser* v. *State of Illinois*, the Supreme Court supported the *Cruikshank* decision. It ruled that the Second Amendment does not bar the state from regulating its citizens' behavior.

The case involved Herman Presser, who had been convicted of operating his own private, unauthorized, armed militia in Illinois. He claimed that the conviction infringed on his right to bear arms. Denying his claim, the Supreme Court ruled that the state had the power to control and regulate military groups:

> **Under our political system . . . [rights] are subject to the regulation and control of the state and federal governments, acting in due regard to their respective prerogatives and powers.**

Courts continue to use both these cases, *Presser v. State of Illinois* and *U.S. v. Cruikshank*, as grounds for ruling that the Second Amendment does not forbid rational gun-control laws.

Militia versus Individual Rights

United States v. Miller is probably the case most cited by other courts to uphold the view that the right to bear arms refers to the militia and is not an individual right. In 1938 Frank Layton and Jack Miller transported an unregistered sawed-off shotgun from Oklahoma to Arkansas. The action was illegal under the National Firearms Act. When the men's case came to court, they argued that the law violated the Constitution. The states, they argued, not the federal government, had the power to police firearms. In addition, they claimed, the law violated their constitutional right to bear arms. When a district court judge in Arkansas agreed, the federal government appealed to the Supreme Court.

The high court made the following rulings:

- **The National Firearms Act did not violate the Constitution or seize power from the state.**

- **Having a sawed-off shotgun has no "reasonable relationship to the preservation or efficiency of a well regulated militia," and there is no evidence that such a weapon "could contribute to the common defense."**

- **Since that is the case, the Second Amendment does not guarantee "the right to keep and bear such an instrument."**

Based on historical records, the court concluded that the word *militia* in the Second Amendment refers to "a body of citizens enrolled for military discipline" who, "when called for service . . . were expected to appear bearing arms supplied by themselves and of the kind in common use at the time."

In addition, the Court stated that none of the "right to bear arms" provisions in state constitutions supported Miller's charges that the law violated his rights.

Gun-rights supporters argue that the Court's definition of militia strengthens their view that individual citizens have a right and a duty to own guns. Gun-control advocates point out that the ruling linked the right to bear arms to a weapon's use in defending the community, not oneself. It did not, they note, authorize gun ownership for individual use.

The Supreme Court issued another ruling on the Second Amendment in 1980 in the case *Lewis* v. *United States*. In 1961 George Lewis Jr. was convicted of a felony, breaking and entering, in Florida. He served a prison term for the offense. In 1977, after he had been released, police in Virginia arrested him and charged him with illegally carrying a firearm. The Gun Control Act of 1968 makes it a crime for felons to own or possess a firearm.

No lawyer represented Lewis at the 1961 trial, which Lewis claimed had violated his right to an attorney. Because his previous conviction was based on a faulty trial, Lewis argued, he should not be considered a felon and the gun charge should be dropped.

The Supreme Court rejected Lewis's claims. In ruling on the case, the Court stated that until a felony charge has been lifted, a felon is barred from owning a gun under the law's provisions. The ruling has significance in the gun-control issue because it upheld the Gun Control Act of 1968 and affirmed that such restrictions on the use of firearms "are neither based upon constitutionally suspect criteria, nor do they trench [infringe] upon any constitutionally protected liberties." Citing Miller, the decision noted that "the Second Amendment guarantees no right to keep and bear a firearm that does not have some reasonable relationship to . . . the preservation or efficiency of a well regulated militia."

The court added that repeated rulings had allowed lawmakers to bar felons from "activities far more fundamental than the possession of a firearm," such as voting, holding office in a labor union, or practicing medicine.

Lower Court Decisions

The collective interpretation of the Second Amendment has also been supported by cases the Supreme Court has refused to hear. One such case, *Quilici* v. *Village of Morton Grove* (1982), sought to overturn that town's law banning private citizens from owning handguns. A federal appeals court upheld the law and ruled that the banned handguns did not qualify as weapons needed by militias. The court also ruled that the Constitution does not include the right to possess handguns for self-defense.

A second case, *United States* v. *Oakes* (1977), involved a man named Ted E. Oakes who had been convicted in a

Kansas district court of illegally owning a machine gun. This violated federal firearms laws. Among other arguments, Oakes claimed that the law violated his right to bear arms. To support his claim, he noted that the Kansas Constitution described the state militia as including all "able-bodied male citizens between the ages of twenty-one and forty-five years." Oakes said he qualified under those terms. He also noted that he was a member of a militia-type organization that was registered with the state.

The appeals court denied Oakes's claims. Quoting the *Miller* decision, the court ruled that "the purpose of the second amendment . . . was to preserve the effectiveness and assure the continuation of the state militia." Furthermore, the court stated, "To apply the amendment so as to guarantee appellant's right to keep an unregistered firearm which has not been shown to have any connection to the militia, merely because he is technically a member of the Kansas militia, would be unjustifiable in terms of either logic or policy."

The appeals court also turned down Oakes's claim that "the right of an individual to bear arms is fundamental." Like the Supreme Court, U.S. appeals courts have generally linked the right to bear arms to the militia. Following the high court's lead, they have consistently ruled that the Second Amendment does not forbid reasonable gun-control laws. They have also taken the stand that the amendment does not guarantee an individual's absolute right to bear arms. By refusing to rule on such cases, the high court let stand lower court rulings that upheld the right of states to regulate firearms.

A New Challenge

A new case that may be headed for the Supreme Court promises to challenge past Court decisions on the Second Amendment. The case, *United States v. Emerson*, attacks a

1996 amendment to Clinton's 1994 crime bill that bans people under a restraining order in domestic violence cases from owning firearms. In August 1998 Timothy and Sacha Emerson were getting a divorce. Timothy Emerson owned a gun. Sacha complained to the police that Timothy had threatened her boyfriend. The local Texas court then issued a restraining order against Timothy Emerson, prohibiting him from threatening Sacha or her friend. The restraining order meant that Emerson could no longer legally own his gun. Several months later a federal grand jury indicted Emerson for violating the gun law.

Before the case went to trial, U.S. District Court Judge Sam Cummings ruled that the gun-law provision violated the "individual right to bear arms." In issuing his decision, Cummings wrote, "There must be a limit to government regulation on lawful firearm possession. This statute exceeds that limit, and therefore it is unconstitutional." He based his decision on the Second and Fifth Amendments.

Cummings's ruling ran counter to more than a century of decisions by the Supreme Court and federal appeals courts. Most previous rulings supported the view that the Constitution does not guarantee a right to bear arms to individuals, but only to states.

A federal appeals court overruled Cummings in the Emerson case, but said that the Second Amendment granted an individual the right to bear arms under "limited, narrowly tailored specific exceptions or restrictions." Under those terms, the decision noted, the federal firearms provision regarding restraining orders was just barely valid. The Supreme Court declined to hear Emerson's appeal in June 2002, but it may reconsider after the case goes to trial.

Gun-control advocates and gun-rights supporters are watching the case closely. A Supreme Court decision supporting the judge's decision could invalidate a number of gun-control laws and deal a serious blow to efforts to limit guns. If the high court rejects the ruling, it would be a major setback for those pushing for gun rights, and an important victory for gun-rights supporters.

States Rights versus Federal Power

Aside from Second Amendment cases, the Court has ruled on the legality of a number of gun-control laws. Some of these cases have pitted federal power against states' rights. In 1995 the Supreme Court ruled that Congress had overstepped its power in passing the Gun-Free School Zones Act of 1990. In a five-to-four decision, the Court struck down the law on the grounds that states, not Congress, have control of public schools under their jurisdiction. The case, *United States* v. *Lopez*, concerned a Texas high school senior named Alfonso Lopez Jr., who brought a handgun and bullets to school. The lower court convicted him of violating the act of 1990, but an appeals court reversed the decision. The case did not address the defendant's right to bear arms. Congress rewrote the law in 1996 to meet the Court's objections.

In 2000 the Supreme Court rejected an appeal filed by gun manufacturers and based on the Lopez decision. The gun makers argued in *Navegar* v. *United States* that interstate commerce regulations did not give Congress the power to ban assault weapons under the 1994 crime bill. President Clinton had argued against the appeal. He said a federal law is needed to control such weapons because local regulations cannot deal with "the nationwide market for firearms."

Another case, involving the Brady Bill, used similar logic. Backed by gun-rights groups, local sheriffs in Arizona and Montana challenged the Brady Bill when it went into effect in 1994. They argued that the federal government lacked the power to force local law-enforcement agencies to check the backgrounds of gun buyers. Again, a divided Court ruled against the federal government. Its decision in the case, *Printz* v. *United States*, said the states did not have to perform background checks. Many continued to do so, however, until the federal check system took over the task in 1998.

Cases against Gun Makers

The courts have increasingly become the new battlefield for gun-control and gun-rights proponents. Hoping to duplicate their success in suing tobacco companies, states and cities have filed more than thirty lawsuits against gun manufacturers since 1998.

New Orleans was the first. On October 30, 1998, the city sued fifteen handgun manufacturers, claiming that they should pay New Orleans for losses caused by guns that did not have lock devices to prevent children and thieves from using the weapons. Other suits quickly followed, filed by Miami-Dade County, Florida; Bridgeport, Connecticut; Atlanta, Georgia; and Cleveland, Ohio, among many others. Some copied the New Orleans charges that gun makers did not equip weapons with safety devices. Other suits charged that manufacturers made it easy for criminals and children to obtain their guns.

In March 2000 Smith & Wesson, the nation's largest gun maker, agreed to a landmark court settlement. Led by President Clinton, the federal government had threatened to join the state and local suits against the company. In exchange for dropping the suits, Smith & Wesson agreed to equip its guns with safety locks. It also said it would require background checks of those who bought the firm's

TOM DIAZ, A SENIOR POLICY ANALYST AT THE VIOLENCE POLICY CENTER AND A STRONG SUPPORTER OF GUN CONTROL, TESTIFIES AT A HEARING CONDUCTED BY THE U.S. SENATE COMMITTEE ON COMMERCE, SCIENCE, AND TRANSPORTATION ON SEPTEMBER 13, 2000. DIAZ CHARGED THAT GUN MANUFACTURERS USED AGGRESSIVE TACTICS—INCLUDING THE TEDDY BEAR SHOWN HERE WITH SMITH & WESSON'S LOGO—TO MARKET GUNS TO CHILDREN.

guns at retail stores and gun shows. In addition, the company agreed to put hidden serial numbers in each gun so that police could trace the weapons more easily.

State and local officials and gun-control groups applauded the Smith & Wesson deal as a step forward in making guns safer. "These cases are not to outlaw guns but to give the industry an opportunity to reform itself," Dennis Henigan of Handgun Control Inc. told the press. "The Smith & Wesson settlement shows that the strategy is working."

Critics charged that the settlement allowed laws to be made through lawsuits instead of by Congress, as the Constitution provided. "The founding fathers would be very sad that laws are now being made by litigation rather than legislation," said Rod Collins of the Michigan Coalition for Responsible Gun Owners. To protest such deals, the group urged Michigan dealers not to buy products from Smith & Wesson.

In April 2000 gun makers fought back, suing twenty-two state and local officials in U.S. District Court in Atlanta. The officials had formed a coalition to force gun makers to adopt safety features and tighten up their distribution system. Those in the coalition pledged to award gun contracts only to those manufacturers who agreed to the code.

Gun makers said the coalition was an attempt to put them out of business. In their lawsuit, they charged that the officials in the coalition had violated the commerce clause of the Constitution and illegally restrained trade. Responding to gun makers' protests, Congress in 2002 considered a bill that would ban lawsuits and other such actions against gun manufacturers and sellers. The proposed bill would have protected gun makers and sellers from liability when their products were used illegally. Thirty states passed similar laws or were considering such legislation. But the House called off a vote on the bill after the string of thirteen sniper shootings in the Washington, D.C., area in October 2002.

Mixed Results

The battle in the courts has produced mixed results. A New York jury in 1999 found nine gun makers guilty of negligence in the deaths of people killed by weapons they manufactured. The case marked the first time gun makers were held accountable for illegal use of their product. The verdict was overturned by an appeals court in 2001. That reversal, however, has not stopped victims from pursuing similar cases.

In California, in the 2001 case of *Merrill* v. *Navegar*, the families of gun victims sued Navegar, a Florida gun manufacturing company, after Gian Luigi Ferri shot and killed nine people including himself using an assault pistol made by the firm. The company had advertised that the gun's finish was "resistant to fingerprints." That claim, critics said, made the gun attractive to criminals.

In its decision, the California Supreme Court ruled that under state law, gun makers could not be blamed for crimes committed by other people. A bill enacted by California in 2002 revised that policy. The new law allows victims to sue gun makers for liability when their products injure or kill. California became the first state to take the action, which repealed laws passed during the 1980s that granted gun makers special immunity from liability suits.

Courts in several other areas, including Chicago, Miami, and Bridgeport, Connecticut, have turned down liability suits by victims against gun makers. Many cases have yet to be resolved. But in an ongoing New York case, filed in 2002, victims of gun violence used information provided for the first time by the ATF to bolster arguments

against gun makers. The data traced guns from manufacturers to gun owners. Attorneys for the victims hoped to
use the information to prove gun makers knew their guns
were being used illegally but failed to intervene. The case
may determine whether gun makers who know about but
do not stop the illegal use of their guns can be held responsible for injuries and deaths caused by their products.

8
School Shootings and Gun-Control Efforts

At 11:19 A.M. on April 20, 1999, two teenage students dressed in black overcoats opened fire on their classmates at Columbine High School in Colorado. Students later reported that the two gunmen laughed as they sprayed bullets randomly around the cafeteria. Several teens were shot as they ate lunch. The shooters roamed the smoke-filled halls, firing from two shotguns, a ten-shot carbine rifle, and a semiautomatic pistol.

Students at the suburban Denver school ran to hide in closets, under tables, and in bathrooms. They listened to the ping of bullets bouncing off lockers outside and the sound of breaking glass. Teachers barricaded terrified teens in their classrooms to protect them. One teacher bled to death waiting for help to reach him.

For four hours students trapped inside the school waited, prayed, and cried. The shooters climbed to the

A STILL IMAGE FROM A SECURITY CAMERA AT COLUMBINE HIGH SCHOOL IN
GOLDEN, COLORADO, SHOWS DYLAN KLEBOLD, RIGHT, AND ERIC HARRIS
DURING THEIR MURDEROUS RAMPAGE ON APRIL 20, 1999, IN WHICH
THEY KILLED TWELVE STUDENTS AND A TEACHER. THE SHOOTERS, WHO
ALSO INJURED TWENTY-THREE STUDENTS BEFORE KILLING THEMSELVES,
USED TWO SHOTGUNS, A TEN-SHOT CARBINE RIFLE, AND A SEMIAUTOMATIC
PISTOL, IN THE BLOODIEST SCHOOL SHOOTING IN U.S. HISTORY.

school's second-floor library. In little more than seven minutes they slaughtered ten students. With SWAT teams outside, the two teens turned the guns on themselves and pulled the trigger. Police, not yet aware of the gunmen's deaths, led stunned groups of students out of the school. The students formed a thin line as they ran from the school building, holding their hands above their heads to show they had no weapons. Police who entered the school later found the bodies of the killers, Dylan Klebold and Eric Harris, seniors at Columbine. Strapped to their chests were enough pipe bombs to burn down the school.

Captured by television cameras and news photographers, the carnage at Columbine filled Americans with horror. One teacher and fourteen students, including the teenage assassins, died; twenty-three were injured. It was the bloodiest school massacre in U.S. history and a scene Americans would not soon forget.

The Focus on Violence

From President Abraham Lincoln's assassination to the attempt on President Ronald Reagan's life, gun violence aimed at public figures has made front-page news in the United States. These incidents and riots arising in Watts (in Los Angeles, California), and other urban ghettos have always momentarily captured the attention of Americans and have sometimes led to calls for gun control.

A series of mass shootings of private citizens and schoolchildren, however, brought the issue of gun violence home to millions of Americans in the 1980s and 1990s. In many of these incidents, gunmen used automatic or semi-automatic weapons to fire off round after round of deadly bullets. These shootings, like no others, showed white, middle-class citizens that they and their children were not safe from guns even in upscale suburban communities and schools.

One of the early shootings occurred on July 18, 1984. James Oliver Huberty, armed with an Uzi submachine gun, a shotgun, and a pistol, fired more than 200 rounds of ammunition into a crowd at a McDonald's restaurant in San Ysidro, California. Before police killed him, Huberty slaughtered twenty-one people and injured nineteen.

Colin Ferguson left six dead and wounded nineteen when he opened fire on commuters riding the Long Island Railroad in 1993. The shooter got his gun—a Ruger P-89 9-mm pistol—legally from a California sporting goods store after waiting fifteen days to buy the weapon. That tragedy drove Carolyn McCarthy, whose husband was killed and son injured in the incident, to run for Congress from New York. She made gun control her main issue and won the election by an unexpectedly large margin, capturing 57 percent of the vote.

Between 1986 and 1999, disgruntled employees staged fourteen shootings at their workplaces, killing and injuring dozens of people. The killers used handguns in nine of these incidents and rifles in the other five. Several bought the guns they used in the shootings legally. A Xerox worker who killed seven co-workers in Hawaii bought and registered his gun and was licensed to carry the weapon.

American schools witnessed their own carnage. In 1988 a woman shot and killed an eight-year-old boy and wounded four other children at an Illinois elementary school before killing herself. That incident and the similar murderous attack on schoolchildren in Stockton, California, in 1989 horrified the nation. Brian Norman, a senior at Fort Hamilton High School, Brooklyn, expressed the views of many students and adults in an article about gun violence published in *Newsday* after the Long Island Railroad shooting. "When kids are afraid to go outside because they may be shot, you know something has to be done," he said.

Even more troubling to Americans were shootings of students by other students. At least ten shooting sprees, including that at Columbine, occurred in America's schools between 1997 and 2001. A teenage shooter in Pearl, Mississippi, stabbed his mother to death in October 1997, then took a rifle to school and shot nine people, killing two. Two months later a high-school student in West Paducah, Kentucky, fired a pistol at classmates holding a prayer circle at the school. Three died and five suffered wounds in that incident. In March of the following year nine students and a teacher were injured and five died when two middle-school boys—aged eleven and thirteen—pulled the school's fire alarm and then shot at those filing out of the building. Yet another school shooting, in May 1998, in Springfield, Oregon, ended with four dead and twenty-five wounded and left the nation reeling. The bloodbath at Columbine in April 1999 pushed an already sickened public to demand action from legislators, police, and community leaders. "Stop the violence" became the new slogan of an alarmed citizenry.

Although the school shootings traumatized America, youth gunning down other youth did not surprise data collectors or minorities living in the inner cities. According to the Violence Policy Center (a private educational foundation), nearly one-third (32.1 percent) of youths under the age of eighteen murdered by handguns were killed by other youths. Black children were seven times as likely as white children to be killed by a handgun. In 1997 death by gun was the second leading cause of death for black children seventeen years old and younger. Despite the school massacres, homicides rarely occurred at schools, particularly those in white neighborhoods. From 1993 to 1998, fewer than 1 percent of gun deaths of children five to nineteen took place in schools, according to a recent report.

Different Reactions

Gun-control supporters and gun-rights advocates had very different reactions to the attacks at schools. Those pushing for gun control pointed to the shootings as prime examples of the need for tougher gun laws. Commenting after a shooting spree in Atlanta, Georgia, claimed thirteen lives, including that of the shooter, Representative Nita M. Lowey (D-N.Y.) said, "This terrible tragedy highlights once again how important it is that we enact meaningful gun-safety legislation. The American people are demanding action."

Those who supported gun rights called for a much different course of action. Many echoed the sentiments of John R. Lott Jr., a leading gun-rights proponent, who argued for less stringent gun laws. According to Lott, bystanders at the shootings could have stopped the killers if they had been armed themselves. In the Pearl, Mississippi, shooting, for example, the assistant principal subdued the sixteen-year-old gunman with a .45-caliber automatic pistol that he kept in his truck parked outside the school.

In February 2000 a six-year-old Michigan boy took a .32-caliber pistol to school and shot and killed a first-grade classmate. The boy found the loaded gun, which had been stolen, in a shoebox in the house where he was staying. The horror of a child so young taking on the role of killer focused attention once more on gun violence.

Shocked into action by the sight of dead and wounded students, Donna Dees-Thomases of Short Hills, New Jersey, a mother and former public-relations specialist, spearheaded a mothers' movement to protest gun violence against children. The organization would later join forces with the

Brady Campaign. The Million Mom March group sponsored a rally of mothers and others in Washington, D.C., that attracted hundreds of thousands of Americans. The Mothers Day 2000 event, held to honor children affected by gun violence, called on Congress to pass tougher gun laws.

Linda Clark, a grandmother from Maine, told a reporter she came to the march because she was "sick and tired" of children dying from gunshots. "I grew up in a hunting family, a family with guns," she said. "We aren't telling anyone to give up their guns—just lock them up. Register them. License yourself. As a mother and grandmother, I am here to say that we love our children more than the NRA loves its guns."

Members of the Million Mom March said that teaching children how to use guns had not solved the problem. They noted that Kip Kinkel's father had given him the 9 mm Glock pistol he later used to shoot his parents and two classmates. As far as they were concerned, he learned his lesson too well.

A small group of protestors at the Million Mom March known as the Second Amendment Sisters focused on gun rights. Orissa Sargent, also a Maine grandmother from a hunting family, said she believed Americans should be allowed to have guns for hunting and for self-defense. "Our Second Amendment rights are so important," she said. "If they would only enforce the laws they have on the books now, people wouldn't be so quick to commit violence with guns." Group members said parents should teach children how to handle guns as a way to prevent deaths instead of relying on government regulations.

The Juvenile Crime Bill

President Clinton continued his efforts to limit guns in a bill the Democrats presented to Congress in 1997. The bill called for child-safety locks on handguns, banned guns for people convicted of violent crimes as youths, and made it more difficult for felons to own guns. As in the past, this juvenile-crime bill stalled in Congress under pressure from gun-rights groups. After the mid-term elections in 1994, the Republicans controlled both houses of Congress.

In November 1997 the president put a temporary stop to the importation of AK-47s, Uzis, and similar weapons. The following April he issued an executive order to continue the ban. That November Clinton signed a bill passed by Congress that required additional prison sentences for felons using guns to commit crimes.

The national agony in the wake of the school shootings plunged a deeply divided Congress into an emotional debate on the causes and cures of gun violence. Clinton urged Congress to support his reintroduced juvenile-crime bill, which contained a number of gun-control proposals. Among them were a ban on large ammunition clips for assault weapons and a provision that would allow buyers to purchase no more than one handgun a month.

A fierce battle raged in the Senate over an amendment to the bill that would require background checks for all buyers at gun sales. Under the Brady Bill, only those buying guns from licensed dealers had to submit to a three-day background check. The amendment aimed at closing loopholes that allowed young people, criminals, and others to obtain guns without a background check. Private gun sales, especially those at gun shows, had come under attack in the media since the multiple shootings at schools and elsewhere. The two teenage gunmen at Columbine had obtained three of the guns used in the shootings from a friend who bought them at a gun show. An estimated 40 percent of sellers at gun shows are not licensed dealers and do not fall under the Brady Bill rules for background checks.

The amendment passed, but only after Vice President Al Gore broke a tie in the Senate.

The final bill passed the Senate on May 21, 1999 by a 73-to-25 vote. Senators approved most of the gun-control measures Clinton had proposed. In addition to the new gun-show rules, the bill required child-safety locks on handguns sold by dealers, made it more difficult for those under eighteen to obtain semiautomatic assault weapons, and banned the import of ammunition for those guns. For these measures to take effect, however, the House would also have to approve them.

Gun-control advocates cheered the passage of the bill in the Senate. They had high hopes that the House would follow suit. Gun-rights advocates, however, redoubled their efforts to kill the bill in the House.

"Not a Game"

During the discussion on the Clinton juvenile-crime bill, House members waded through forty-four amendments on the entertainment industry and other cultural issues and eleven on gun control. Because of the lengthy debate, House members did not look at the gun-control portion of Clinton's proposals until late in the day on June 17, 1999. Discussion became heated as House members debated competing bills on gun shows. Carolyn McCarthy, now a Democratic representative from New York, proposed an amendment like the one the Senate had approved. It required private sellers at gun shows to follow the same background check system that dealers used under the Brady Bill.

McCarthy begged the House to support her bill. "I am trying to stop the criminals from being able to get guns. That is all I am trying to do," she said. "This is not a game to me. This is not a game to the American people."

Representative William McCollum (R-Fla.) opposed McCarthy's bill as being "overly broad." He urged the

Gun Laws and Teens

Gun laws in the United States vary widely from state to state. Local regulations can be even more diverse. Some states, like Massachusetts and New York, require gun owners to have a license to own or buy handguns. New York City regulations go further, requiring a permit to buy rifles and shotguns as well as handguns. Montana, Maine, and many other states allow people to own and buy handguns, rifles, and shotguns without permits or licenses. Washington, D.C., requires background checks for all gun sales, including those by private individuals. In some areas, no one under twenty-one can own a gun. Other locales allow eighteen-year-olds to have firearms. Morton Grove, a small village in Illinois, bans handguns altogether.

States and municipalities can enact gun laws that are stricter than federal laws. In cases where there is no law or the law is less strict, the federal law applies. Many laws ban the sale of firearms to criminals, children, and people who have histories of severe mental illness.

Federal gun laws make it illegal for licensed dealers to sell handguns to anyone under twenty-one and rifles and shotguns to people younger than eighteen. Those eighteen and older can buy handguns from private sellers and unlicensed dealers at gun shows or private homes. People of any age can own rifles and shotguns, and there is no age restriction on their sales by unlicensed dealers or private sellers.

People of any age can buy assault rifles, assault shotguns, and ammunition clips manufactured before 1994 from private sellers or unlicensed dealers. A person must be eighteen or older to buy such weapons legally from a dealer.

Older model semiautomatic pistols (manufactured before 1994) fall under the same requirements as handguns.

The Brady Bill requires federally licensed dealers to submit names of all gun buyers to federal authorities for a background check. Buyers must wait three business days to allow time for officials to determine if they can legally own a gun. People buying guns from unlicensed dealers or private sellers do not have to undergo a background check.

House to vote against the bill. "It would turn gatherings of friends into gun shows. It would turn neighborhood yard sales into gun shows. . . . It would force gun promoters to really go out of business," he said.

Representative John Dingell (D-Mich.) countered with a watered-down version of the gun-show amendment. Under pressure from Clinton, Dingell had voted for the assault-weapons ban in 1994, a move he later regretted. Dingell believed that gun-rights supporters had voted Democrats out of office the following November, turning control of the House over to the Republicans.

Dingell's amendment required private sellers at gun shows to submit buyers' names for background checks but allowed only twenty-four hours for law-enforcement agencies to complete their investigations. The Dingell proposal would have weakened the Brady Bill by reducing the time for a background check for gun-show dealers (who fell under the three-day background check) as well as private sellers. Under the proposal, background checks would be required only at gun shows with fifty or more firearms on display and with ten or more sellers.

The two amendments headed for a vote on June 17, 1999. Lobbying for and against both bills continued late into the night. Forty-five Democrats—mostly from gun-rights areas of the West and the South—lined up with Republicans to back the Dingell proposal. Some moderate Republicans stood with McCarthy to support her amendment. Finally, shortly after midnight, the House voted by a narrow margin to approve Dingell's measure and to defeat McCarthy's. *The New York Times* called the House actions "a stunning victory for the National Rifle Association."

In later action the House tacked on measures to the final bill that both supported gun control and opposed it. Members approved gun-control advocates' call for safety locks on handguns and a ban on imported ammunition clips. But they eased gun restrictions on residents in Washington, D.C., by allowing them to have loaded handguns in their homes. The House turned down a proposal to raise the minimum age for all handgun buyers from eighteen to twenty-one.

All the amendments, including Dingell's, ultimately failed, however, when the House defeated the juvenile-crime bill to which they were attached. In the complex maneuvering over the issue, Democrats who favored tough gun-control measures voted with Republicans who opposed all gun control to kill the bill.

Congress ended the session without passing any of the gun-control measures advocates had promoted. Democrats hoped Congress's lack of action on gun control would convince voters to elect them and support their candidate for president in 2000, Al Gore.

Several polls conducted in 1999 and 2000 showed that the majority of voters favored tougher gun laws, including safety locks, background checks, gun registration, limits on handguns, and a ban on assault weapons. But the polls also showed that voters did not necessarily identify the Democratic party as the one to accomplish those goals. When asked which party best reflected their views on the issue, voters rated the Democrats only slightly higher than the Republicans. Neither party won support from a majority of those polled. In one poll conducted by CBS News and *The New York Times*, voters rated George W. Bush—who was strongly backed by the NRA—slightly higher than Al Gore as the candidate they agreed with more on the issue of gun control.

Voters also said that, although gun control was important to them, it was only one of many issues they considered when voting for president.

9
Gun Control Today

After an election too close to call, George W. Bush became president only after a ruling by the Supreme Court stopped a recount of disputed ballots in Florida. Once in office, the Bush administration made it clear which side of the gun-control debate it favored. In a letter to the NRA in 2001, Attorney General John Ashcroft sided with gun-rights proponents' arguments that the Second Amendment grants individuals the right to bear arms. Ashcroft, as attorney general, sets policy for the Justice Department, which he heads. President Bush has also supported that position. While previous presidents have held similar views, federal policy has generally not endorsed the view that the Second Amendment guarantees an individual's right to own a gun.

If Americans support gun control, why do they elect

politicians who oppose it? Gun-rights advocates contend that the polls are poorly worded, misleading, or just plain wrong. A recent poll conducted by ABC offers another explanation: Americans support gun-control laws, but they don't think the measures work. According to the poll, 63 percent of Americans favor stricter gun-control laws. But only about half of those polled said they thought gun control would reduce violent crime.

Does Gun Control Work?

Often major gun legislation follows a catastrophic event, such as the assassination of President Kennedy in 1963. But do the laws that are passed address the real problem? Do gun-control laws work? Does reducing the number of guns available also reduce the number of gun-related crimes? The good news is that, while still high, gun violence and gun-related crime rates in the United States have been decreasing steadily since the early 1990s. Deaths due to murder by gun dropped by almost half from 1993 to 1998. Suicides and accidental deaths caused by firearms have also declined.

A police crackdown on criminals, tougher jail terms for those using guns to commit crimes, and a reduction in crack cocaine traffic have helped reduce gun murders. Efforts to educate children and adults about gun safety, gun-control laws that have helped make it more difficult to obtain firearms, gun safety measures, and fewer guns being manufactured have also been credited for the decline in deaths and injuries.

U.S. government statistics show a strong relationship between guns and crime. Almost two-thirds of the murders committed in the United States in 2000 were carried out by people using guns. In the group at highest risk for homicides—

SUPPORTERS OF GUN RIGHTS PROTEST AGAINST GUN CONTROL IN AUSTIN, TEXAS. THOSE WHO OPPOSE GUN CONTROL MEASURES ARGUE THAT TOUGHER LAWS SHOULD BE AIMED AT CRIMINALS, NOT AGAINST HONEST CITIZENS WHO OWN GUNS.

black males fifteen to twenty-four years old—nearly nine out of ten of the murders in 2000 involved firearms.

Government data suggest that some gun-control laws have had positive results. A joint report by the ATF, the Department of Justice, and the Department of the Treasury show that since 1994 the Brady Bill has stopped more than 250,000 illegal gun sales.

In another study, medical researchers in California examined laws that made it difficult for people convicted of violent crimes to get guns. The research showed that fewer people were arrested for violent crimes after the policy was adopted.

Critics of gun control say laws restricting guns don't work. Most criminals, they say, get guns despite the Brady Bill and similar laws. A survey of state prisoners conducted by the Justice Department in 1997 showed that 80 percent had obtained guns from family, friends, or an illegal source.

Gun-control opponents point to a 1998 study comparing states that had waiting periods and background checks before the Brady Bill went into effect and those that did not. The study concluded that the Brady Bill reduced the number of suicides among older Americans. But

A TOURIST LOOKS AT THE APPROXIMATELY 18,000 PAIRS OF SHOES REPRESENTING VICTIMS OF GUN VIOLENCE ON DISPLAY NEAR THE LIBERTY BELL IN PENNSYLVANIA ON JULY 29, 2000, AT A PROTEST DURING THE REPUBLICAN NATIONAL CONVENTION. THE DISPLAY WAS ORGANIZED BY THE SILENT MARCH, A NATIONAL GRASSROOTS GUN CONTROL ORGANIZATION.

adoption of the Brady Bill did not seem to make much difference in the rates of homicide and suicide among younger Americans. The study's authors noted, however, that guns from private sales, thefts, and other means not covered by the Brady Bill may have influenced the results.

More Guns, Less Crime?

Robert Shockey reacted quickly when two masked robbers entered a video store in Orange City, Florida, where his son worked. When one robber aimed a rifle at him, Shockey pulled out his .45-caliber handgun and shot and killed the nineteen-year-old man. Shockey then wounded the other robber as he grabbed for the rifle.

"I feel bad about what happened," Shockey, who had a concealed-weapon permit for the gun, told a reporter later.

"I had to do it; I didn't have any choice. I had to defend myself and the people around me."

Critics of gun control contend that armed citizens help fight crime. Shockey's case is one of many they say prove that point. Gun-rights advocates have often used studies by professor Gary Kleck and economist John Lott to show that areas where residents are allowed to carry concealed weapons have far less crime. However, Lott's work has recently been called into question because he failed to produce the data on which he based his results.

A new study, conducted by John Donohue III of Stanford Law School and Ian Ayres of Yale Law School, found that the biggest drops in both murder rates and robbery rates occurred in states that did not allow private citizens to carry concealed guns. In a few cases, certain crimes decreased in areas with concealed-weapon permits, but for the most part the reverse occurred. If the findings are confirmed, the 2002 report could strengthen the argument for gun control.

Health and Safety

Gun-control advocates and public-health groups have recently focused more attention on product safety and health issues involving guns. These groups are pushing for safety requirements for gun makers. Imported firearms have to meet federal standards on safety and quality. There are no federal laws, however, that require U.S. gun makers to do the same.

These groups also favor safety locks and regulations that require gun owners to keep weapons locked up and away from children and those with mental or emotional problems. "The only effective way to treat a gunshot wound is to keep it from happening in the first place," said Dr. Garen Wintemute, a physician who treats emergency room patients.

NRA vice president Wayne LaPierre has voiced support for safety locks and trigger locks. But he has said such safety features should be voluntary. Training children and first-time shooters in gun safety is more effective in preventing accidental deaths, he believes.

Some gun-rights supporters oppose safety requirements because such features will increase the cost of guns. They also fear that people in danger may be killed before they can remove the safety lock from their gun.

Charges of Bias

The issue of gun control is so complicated that it demands careful, scientific study. But what research, and which figures, should one believe? Both sides of the gun-control issue provide numbers "proving" their arguments. In many cases, however, the studies have been designed to favor one side of the argument and ignore facts that support opposing views. Even data collected by the U.S. government have been questioned as being biased.

People on both sides of the gun-control debate charge that statistics and other data are biased. Dr. Timothy Wheeler, who founded Doctors for Responsible Gun Ownership, said medical journals too often use "advocacy research"—studies undertaken to support a certain viewpoint. "They advocated getting rid of guns and enacting laws against law-abiding gun owners," he said. "Then they backed it up with advocacy research."

On the other side of the issue, many researchers have questioned the studies on the use of guns for self-defense conducted by John Lott and Gary Kleck.

"Many of the basic statistics about guns are in wide disagreement with each other," said researcher Philip J. Cook. "That's been a real puzzle to people who are trying to understand what's going on."

The only way to resolve differing interpretations of data and study results, according to an article in the *Journal of the American Medical Association*, is to conduct more research. Gun policy should not be based on theory, the article suggests, but "on empirical evidence of what works." Other analysts call on the news media to do its part by checking data and study results before reporting them as fact.

The past president of the American Medical Association, Dr. Richard F. Corlin, laments that the medical community cannot answer vital questions about violent deaths in America because of the lack of credible data. He faults elected leaders for not providing the money to fund research into gun violence. "Gun violence is a threat to the public health of our country," Corlin said. "This is a fact. Not a political statement. And we will not be able to effectively address the problem—without current, consistent, and credible data."

The American Medical Association, the Centers for Disease Control, medical researchers, and other public health groups are pushing for a national reporting system on injuries caused by firearms. A report issued in 1999 by a handgun-control group noted that the United States does a better job reporting polio, which has affected only 137 Americans since 1980, than it does tracking injuries caused by firearms.

Working toward a Solution

Filmmaker Michael Moore is among those who believe the best way to reduce gun violence is to eliminate the need for guns. Moore, whose documentary *Bowling for Columbine* focuses on gun violence, thinks many Americans own guns because they are afraid. This fear has spread, Moore contends, because the media play up crimes of violence, making it seem that every person is in danger, when in fact such crimes have been declining. Accurate news coverage, Moore argues, would go a long way toward easing Americans' fears and lessening their reliance on guns for self-defense. The way to cut crime even more, he says, is to improve living conditions in inner cities where crime is highest. "If we lived in a society that said our first goal was employment at a livable wage for everyone, if the person living next door to you—if that person's making $40,000 a year, what's the chance they're going to come in and steal your TV or harm you on the street? Absolutely none."

At present, however, policymakers continue their attempts to reduce gun deaths through other means. A 2002 report on youth gun violence funded by the Packard Foundation calls on the American public and state and federal governments to work together to address the problem. The study's authors note that a program to prevent deaths and injuries in motor vehicles used education, strict safety standards, and tougher laws and enforcement to save an estimated 243,400 lives between 1966 and 1990.

A similar approach, they say, could work to curb gun deaths. Among the strategies recommended are:

- tight regulations on gun quality, design, and safety features;
- a commitment by parents to keep guns away from children;
- community programs to keep neighborhoods safe and to emphasize that gun violence is not acceptable;
- tougher restrictions on the sale and possession of guns.

The last point in particular angers gun-rights supporters. The report recommends that gun owners be licensed, guns be registered, and laws enacted to make it more difficult for children and teens to obtain firearms. Constitutional lawyer Kurt Kluin and others make a case for limiting handguns voluntarily. Effective gun control, Kluin says, depends "on the voluntary cooperation of gun owners." Prohibition failed because the American public did not support it. According to ABC's poll, a large majority of Americans favor many gun-control efforts. Even those groups most likely to support gun rights—men, Republicans, and gun owners—favored all the gun-control measures in the poll except bans on concealed weapons and handgun sales.

The polls also show that more than half of handgun owners bought their weapon to defend themselves and their property. Kluin notes that rifles are much more effective for self-defense than handguns. He and others have suggested that handgun owners might be convinced to swap their small guns for rifles if they knew the facts. That might be one way, he says, to reduce the number of guns that criminals could steal and hide easily.

The Packard report's authors acknowledge that it may be hard to find strategies that both sides of the gun-control issue can agree on. But without a plan, they warn, American children and adults "will continue to die, unnecessarily and senselessly, from gunshot wounds."

Advocates on both sides find it unacceptable that so many Americans, especially children, are shot to death. "Hopefully," the report's authors note, "that point of agreement can serve as the foundation for aggressive efforts to reduce youth gun violence in the United States."

Notes

Chapter 1

p. 9, par. 3, Brady, Sarah. "Statement by Sarah Brady on the Sniper Shootings," press release from the Brady Campaign to Prevent Gun Violence, October 8, 2002.

p. 9, par. 5, Barnes, Michael D. "Brady Campaign/MMM Stress Importance of Creating a National Ballistics Firearms Database," press release from the Brady Campaign to Prevent Gun Violence, October 17, 2002.

p. 10, par. 2, Butterfield, Fox. "Despite Violations, U.S. Let Gun Shop in Sniper Case Stay Open, Records Show," *The New York Times*, December 9, 2002.

p. 10, par. 3, LaPierre, Wayne, and Chris W. Cox. "Joint Statement on Ballistic 'Fingerprinting,'" National Rifle Association/NRA Institute for Legislative Action, October 17, 2002.

p. 10, par. 3, Woodruff, Judy. "Sniper on the Loose: A Campaign Issue?," CNN, October 22, 2002.

p. 11, par. 2, National Vital Statistics Reports, vol. 51, no. 5, March 14, 2003, p. 17.

p. 11, par. 2, Web–based Injury Statistics Query and Reporting System (WISQARS), National Center for Injury Control and Prevention. http://www.cdc.gov/ncipc/wisqars/default.htm (Accessed October 10, 2002.)

pp. 12–13, The Seventh United Nations Survey of Crime Trends, 1998–2000; Uniform Crime Reporting Program (U.S.).

p. 16, par. 2–3, Stolinsky, David C. "America: The Most Violent Nation?," *Medical Sentinel*, vol. 5, no. 6, November/December 2000.

p. 17, par. 4, "Uniform Crime Reports, Crime in the United States—1995," Federal Bureau of Investigation, p. 274.

p. 17, par. 4, "Commerce in Firearms," Department of the Treasury, Bureau of Alcohol, Tobacco & Firearms, February 2000, p. 6.

p. 17, par. 5, Duggan, Mark. "More Guns, More Crime," Cambridge, MA: National Bureau of Economic Research, 2000.

p. 18, Kellermann, Arthur, et al. "Gun Ownership as a Risk Factor for Homicide in the Home," *The New England Journal of Medicine*, vol. 329, no. 15, October 7, 1993, pp. 1084–1091.

p. 18, par. 1, Kellermann, Arthur, et al. "Injuries and deaths due to firearms in the home," *Journal of Trauma*, 45(2), August 1998, pp. 263–267.

p. 18, par. 2, "Boy, 4, accidentally kills," *Florida Times-Union*, April 9, 2002.

p. 18, par. 4, Cook, P. J., and J. Ludwig. *Gun Violence: The Real Costs*, New York: Oxford University Press,

2000, p. 113; cited in "Factsheet" Firearm Injury and Death in the United States," Baltimore, MD: Johns Hopkins University, 2002.

pp. 18–19, Heston, Charlton. Speech to National Press Club, September 14, 1997.

p. 19, par. 1, Kleck, Gary, and Don B. Kates. *Armed: New Perspectives on Gun Control*, Amherst, NY: Prometheus Books, 2001, p. 15.

p. 19, par. 2, Flynn, Kevin. "Man Kills Intruder," *The New York Times*, February 11, 2003.

pp. 20–21, Interview with author, Sept. 18, 2002.

p. 22, par. 1, "Suing Gun Manufacturers: Hazardous to Our Health," Policy Report No. 223, March 1999, National Center for Policy Analysis, Washington, D.C.

p. 22, par. 1, "REMPAC Overview," Remington Arms Co. Inc. Political Action Committee, Greensboro, N.C., 2002.

p. 23, O'Brien, Gwen. "Boy's action 'justifiable': 11-year-old shoots, kills assailant," *South Bend Tribune*, February 6, 2002.

p. 24, par. 1, Bureau of Justice Statistics. "Guns and Crime, Crime Data Brief," NCJ–147003, April 1994.

p. 24, par. 1, Murray, Iain. "The U.S. Gun–control Debate: A Critical Look," Statistical Assessment Service, Washington, D.C., 2001.

Chapter 2

p. 25, Second Amendment, The Bill of Rights, U.S. Constitution.

p. 26, par. 2, Articles of Confederation, Article VI.

p. 26, par. 3, Virginia Constitution, Art. I, § 13 (1776).

p, 26, par. 3, Tennessee Constitution, Art. XI, §26 (1796).

p. 26, par. 3, Pennsylvania Constitution, Art. IX, § 21 (1790).

p. 26, par. 3, Volokh, Eugene. "State Constitutional Right

to Keep and Bear Arm Provisions," UCLA School of Law
http://www1.law.ucla.edu/~volokh/beararms/
statecon.htm (Accessed June 3, 2003.)

p. 29, "The Bill of Rights: A Brief History," ACLU
Briefing Paper, No. 9.

pp. 30–31, Volokh, Eugene. "Testimony of Eugene Volokh
on the Second Amendment," Senate Subcommittee on
the Constitution, September. 23, 1998.

p. 31, par. 2, Willing, Richard. "Case could shape future
of gun control," *USA Today: Nation*, August 27, 1999.

Chapter 3

pp. 33–34, 36, 37, DeConde, Alexander. *Gun Violence in
America: The Struggle for Control.* Boston: Northeastern
Univeristy Press, 2001, p. 19.

p. 37, par. 2, "A Brief History of NRA," National Rifle
Association, Fairfax, Va.

p. 38, par. 1, "Noncombatant's Guide to the Gun Control
Fight," *The Issue of Gun Control.* New York: H. W.
Wilson Co., 1981, p. 40.

p. 38, par. 1, DeConde, Alexander. *Gun Violence in
America*, p. 95.

p. 38, par. 1, "Commerce in Firearms," Department of the
Treasury, Bureau of Alcohol, Tobacco & Firearms,
February 2000, pp. A–3, A–5.

p. 38, par. 1, Riczo, Steven. "Guns, America, and the 21st
Century (laws evaluation)," *USA Today* (magazine),
March 2001.

p. 38, par. 2, Thurman, Russ. "Firearms Production,"
Shooting Industry, July 2000.

Chapter 4

pp. 39–40, Kluin, Kurt. "Gun Control: Is it a
Legal and Effective Means of Controlling Firearms in

the United States?" *Washburn Law Journal*, vol. 21, 1982, footnote 87.

p. 40, par. 3, Burger, Warren. The MacNeil/Lehrer NewsHour, PBS, December 16, 1991.

p. 41, DeConde, Alexander. *Gun Violence in America*, pp. 21, 23.

p. 43, par. 1. Foner, Eric, ed. "Nat Turner," Englewood Cliffs, NJ, Prentice-Hall: 1971, p. 115. Cited in Cramer, Clayton E. "The Racist Roots of Gun Control," *Kansas Journal of Law & Public Policy*, winter 1995, p. 17.

p. 43, par. 1, Thorpe, Francis Newton. "The Federal and State Constitutions, Colonial Charters, and Other Organic Laws of the States, Territories, and Colonies Now or Heretofore Forming The United States of America," Washington: Government Printing Office, 1909. Cited in Cramer, Clayton E. "The Racist Roots of Gun Control."

p. 43, par. 1, *State* v. *Newsom*, 5 Iredell 181, 27 N.C. 250 (1844). Cited in Cramer, Clayton E. "The Racist Roots of Gun Control."

p. 43, par. 2, "An American Time Capsule: Three Centuries of Broadsides and Other Printed Ephemera," Historical Collections for the National Digital Library, "American Memory" collection.

p. 44, par. 1, Fourteenth Amendment, U.S. Constitution.

p. 44, par. 2, "African-Americans in South Carolina: Reconstruction, Restoration—1865–1900." South Carolina Information Highway. http://www.sciway.net/afam/reconstruction/blackcodes.html (Accessed October 2, 2002.)

p. 44, par. 2, Tunnell, Ted. *Crucible of Reconstruction*. Baton Rouge, LA: Louisiana State University Press, 1984), p. 157. Cited in DeConde, p. 75.

p. 44–45, par. 1, "Noncombatant's Guide to the Gun Control Fight," p. 40.

p. 45, par. 2, DeConde, Alexander. *Gun Violence in America*, pp. 106–107.

p. 45, par. 3, Texas Livestock Journal (Fort Worth), February 1882. Cited in DeConde, p. 85.

p. 46, par. 1–2, DeWan, George. "Guns & History: Fourth of a Series," *Newsday*, December 9, 1993.

pp. 46–47, par. 1 "For a Better Enforcement of the Law," *American Bar Association Journal*, vol. 8, 1922, p. 590–591, cited in DeConde.

p. 48, par. 1, "The Uniform Firearms Act," *Virginia Law Review*, vol. 18, 1932, p. 904.

p. 48, par. 3, Geringer, Joseph. "George 'Bugs' Moran: His War With Al Capone." Cited in "Return to the Scene of the Crime—Chicago" by Richard Lindberg.

p. 49, DeConde, Alexander. *Gun Violence in America*, p. 128.

Chapter 5

p. 53, DeConde, Alexander. *Gun Violence in America*, p. 155.

pp. 54–55, Zimring, Franklin E. "Firearms and Federal Law: The Gun Control Act of 1968," *Journal of Legal Studies*, vol. 4, 1975, pp. 144–145.

p. 54, par. 2, DeConde, Alexander. *Gun Violence in America*, p. 167

p. 54, par. 2, "Commerce in Firearms in the United States," Department of the Treasury, Bureau of Alcohol, Tobacco & Firearms, p. A–5.

p. 54, par. 3, "Homicide trends in the U.S.," U.S. Department of Justice, Bureau of Justice Statistics, 1950–1970.

p. 55, DeConde, Alexander. *Gun Violence in America*, p. 171.

p. 57, par. 2, Ibid., 176.

p. 57, par. 3, "Where the NRA stands on gun legislation," *The American Rifleman*, March 1968, p. 22.

p. 59, par. 1, 2, Alexander DeConde, *Gun Violence in America*, p. 185.

p. 59, par. 3–4, Report of the National Commission on the Causes and Prevention of Violence, December 10, 1969.

p. 58, 114 Congressional Record 14773 (1968).

pp. 60–63, The Gun Control Act of 1968, Public Law 90–618.

p. 63, par. 1, "Commerce in Firearms in the United States," p. 5.

p. 63, par. 2, "Table 1: Federal Firearms Law Cases Recommended for Prosecution, Indictment and Convictions by Fiscal Year, 1965–73." U.S. Department of Treasury, Bureau of Alcohol, Tobacco and Firearms, Statistics Division. Cited in Zimring, p. 159.

p. 63, par. 3, Zimring, Franklin E. "Firearms and Federal Law: The Gun Control Act of 1968," p. 161.

p. 64, par. 2, p. 181, Table 7, source: Bureau of Alcohol, Tobacco and Firearms, Project I (1974).

pp. 65–66. Oliver, Jim. "Washington Report," *Guns and Ammo*, vol. 23, no. 6, May 1979, in *The Issue of Gun Control*, New York: H. W. Wilson Co., 1981, p. 115.

pp. 66–67, Kluin, Kurt. "Gun Control: Is it a Legal and Effective Means of Controlling Firearms in the United States?"

p. 67, par. 3, Presidential Campaign Debate between Gerald R. Ford and Jimmy Carter, October 22, 1976.

Chapter 6

p. 75, par. 3,"Long-Term Contribution Trends," 1990–2002, Center for Responsive Politics, Washington, D.C.

p. 76, Prud'Homme. Alex. "A Blow to The N.R.A.: The House takes an overdue stand for gun control," *Time*, May 20, 1991.

p. 77, par. 1, Reagan, Ronald. "Why I'm For the Brady Bill,"

The New York Times, March 29, 1991, p. A21:3. Cited in DeConde, p. 242.

p. 77, par. 2, Prud'Homme, Alex. "A Blow to The N.R.A."

p. 78–79, Congressional Record, 102nd Congress.

p. 81, "Crime Bill Squeaks By in Senate, Several Republicans Join the Democrats to Send the $30 Billion Program to President Clinton," *Portland Press Herald*, August 26, 1994, p. 1A.

p. 82, par. 2, "Congress' Crime Bill Ends Up a Mixed Bag, It's Neither as Good as Democrats Claim, nor as Bad as Republicans Say," *Portland Press Herald*, August 27, 1994, p. 8A.

p. 82, par. 4, Outpost of Freedom, *Sentinel*, vol. II, no. 2, March 8, 1995.

p. 82, par. 5, Abrams, Jim. "NRA Official Defends Anti-Federal Agent Rhetoric," Associated Press, April 30, 1995.

Chapter 7

p. 84, par. 2, ABA Task Force on Gun Violence, Report to the House of Delegates (1994).

p. 85, *United States* v. *Cruikshank*, 92 U.S. 542 (1875), 92 U.S. 542.

p. 86, *Presser* v. *State of Illinois*, 116 U.S. 252 (1886).

pp. 86–87, *United States* v. *Miller*, 307 U.S. 174 (1939), 307 U.S. 174.

pp. 87–88, *Lewis* v. *United States*, 445 U.S. 55 (1980).

pp. 88–89, *United States* v. *Oakes*, 564 F.2d 384 (10th Cir 1977).

pp. 89–90, U.S. District Judge Sam R. Cummings, *United States* v. *Emerson*, Federal Supplement 2nd Series v. 46, p. 598 (Northern District of Texas, April 7, 1999).

p. 90, Greenhouse, Linda. "Justices Reject Cases on Right

to Bear Arms," *The New York Times*, June 11, 2002.

p. 91, Greenhouse, Linda. "Supreme Court Roundup; Justices' Decisions Shape New Course for U.S. Sentencing," *The New York Times*, October 3, 2000.

p. 94, Chebium, Raju. "Litigation moving gun–control issue into courts," CNN Online. (Accessed October 9, 2002.)

Chapter 8

pp. 97–99, "Inside Columbine," *Rocky Mountain News* http://www.rockymountainnews.com/drmn/columbine (Accessed June 3, 2003.)

p. 100, "Pistol Bought Legally, Says California Dealer," http://www.rockymountainnews.com/drmn/columbine *Chicago Sun Times*, December 9, 1993, p. 7.

p. 101, par. 1, DeWan, George. "Guns & History: Fourth of a Series."

p. 101, par. 3, "Kids in the Line of Fire: Children, Handguns, and Homicide, 2001," The Violence Policy Center.

pp. 101–102, Lois A. Fingerhut and Katherine K. Christoffel, "Firearm–Related Death and Injury among Children and Adolescents," *The Future of Children*, vol. 12, no. 2, 2002, summer/fall 2002, pp. 25–37.

p. 102, par. 2, Stout, David. "Shootings in Atlanta: The Capitol; Gun Control Awaits Action By Conferees," *The New York Times*, July 30, 1999.

p. 102, par. 3, Lott, John R. "Concealed guns reduce crime; If people are packing, crooks think twice," *Star Tribune* (Minneapolis, MN), August 16, 1998.

p. 102, par. 3, "Town tries to cope with school shooting," Associated Press in *Lubbock Avalanche-Journal*, October 10, 1997.

p. 103, Mack, Sharon. "Maine Moms March," *Bangor Daily News*, May 18, 2000.

p. 104, "Where'd They Get Their Guns? An Analysis of the Firearms Used in High-Profile Shootings, 1963 to 2001," Violence Policy Center report, April 2001.

pp. 105, 108, Congressional Record, 106th Congress, June 17, 1999, p. H4605.

p. 108, "State Gun Laws," NRA Institute for Legislative Action, http://nraila.org/GunLaws.asp? FormMode=state (Accessed September 17, 2002.)

pp. 108–107, "State Laws and Published Ordinances— Firearms," Department of the Treasury, Bureau of Alcohol, Tobacco and Firearms, 22nd Edition, http://www.atf.treas.gov/firearms/statelaws/22edition.htm (Accessed September 17, 2002.)

p. 108, par. 2, Dao, James. "Guns and Schools: The Democrats; Michigan Lawmaker's Agenda Highlights a Split," *The New York Times*, June 18, 1999.

p. 108, par. 4, Mitchell, Alison, and Frank Bruni. "Guns and Schools: The Overview; House Vote Deals a Stinging Defeat to Gun Controls," *The New York Times*, June 18, 1999.

p. 109, CBS News/New York Times Poll, May 10–13, 2000.

Chapter 9

p. 111, par. 1, ABC News/New York Times Poll, May 10–13, 2000.

p. 111, par. 2, National Vital Statistics Report, vol. 49, no. 8, September 21, 2001, p. 10.

pp. 111–112, "Leading Causes of Violence–Related Injury Deaths, United States 2000," National Center for Injury Control and Prevention, Atlanta, Georgia.

p. 112, par. 2, "Gun Shows: Brady Checks and Crime Gun

Traces," Department of the Treasury, Department of Justice, and Bureau of Alcohol, Tobacco, and Firearms, January 1999, p. 1.

p. 112, par. 3, Cole, Thomas B. "Complementary Strategies to Prevent Firearm Injury," *Journal of the American Medical Association*, vol. 285, no. 8, February 28, 2001.

p. 112, par. 4, "1997 Survey of State Prison Inmates," U.S. Department of Justice, Bureau of Justice Statistics.

pp. 113–114 "Store Worker's Dad Shoots Two Robbers," Associated Press, in the *Tallahassee Democrat*, March 20, 2002, p. B5.

pp. 115–116, Phalen, Kathleen. "Target prevention: Researching the epidemiology of gun violence," *American Medical News*, August 20, 2001.

p. 115, par. 2, LaPierre, Wayne. NRA Annual Meeting address, May 1, 1999.

p. 116, par. 1–2, Iain, Murray. "The U.S. Gun-control Debate: A Critical Look, Statistical Assessment Service, 2001.

p. 116, par. 3, Cole, Thomas B. "Complementary Strategies to Prevent Firearm Injury."

p. 116, par. 4, Corlin, Richard F., M.D., "Reducing gun violence," *American Medical News*, June 29, 2002.

p. 116, par. 5, "Another good idea on firearms," *Milwaukee Journal Sentinel*, February 15, 1999. Cited in Deborah Azrael, Catherine Barber, and David Hemenway, "A Call to Arms for a National Reporting System on Firearm Injuries," Harvard Injury Control Research Center, April 28, 2000.

p. 117, par. 1, "Interview by Phil Donahue of Michael Moore," MSNBC, October 28, 2002.

p. 117, par. 2–3, Bonnie, F. J., C. E. Fulcro, and C. T. Liverman. "Reducing the burden of injury: Advancing prevention and treatment," Washington, DC: National Academy Press, 1999. Quoted in "Children, Youth, and Gun Violence," *The Future of Children*, vol. 12, no. 2, 2002, p. 19.

p. 118, par. 1–2, Kluin, Kurt. "Gun Control: Is it a Legal and Effective Means of Controlling Firearms in the United States?," p. 265.

p. 118, par. 1, Merkle, Daniel. "Ambivalence on Gun Control," ABCNEWS Polling Unit, Sept. 8, 2001.

p. 118, par. 2–4, Reich, Kathleen, Patti Culross, and Richard Behrman. "Children, Youth, and Gun Violence," *The Future of Children*, vol. 12, no. 2, 2002, p. 19.

Further Information

Further Reading

Adams, Maggi. *Should We Have Gun Control?*
Minneapolis, MN: Lerner Publications, 1991.

Croft, Jennifer. *Everything You Need to Know about Guns in the Home.* New York: Rosen Group, 2000.

Gottfried, Ted. *Gun Control: Public Safety & the Right to Bear Arms.* Brookfield, CT: Millbrook Press, 1993.

Hanson, Freya Ottem. *The Second Amendment: The Right to Own Guns.* Springfield, NJ: Enslow, 1998.

Roleff, Tamara L. *Guns & Crime.* San Diego, CA: Greenhaven Press, 2000.

Sommers, Michael. *The Right to Bear Arms: Individual Rights & Civic Responsibility.* New York: Rosen Group, 2000.

Web Sites

American Civil Liberties Union
http://www.aclu.org

Brady Campaign to Prevent Gun Violence
http://www.bradycampaign.org

Doctors for Responsible Gun Ownership
http://www.claremont.org/projects/doctors/index.html

Emory Center for Injury Control
http://www.sph.emory.edu/CIC/

Federal Bureau of Investigation Uniform Crime Reports
http://www.fbi.gov/ucr/ucr.htm

GunCite
http://www.guncite.com/

Join Together
http://www.jointogether.org/

Keep and Bear Arms
http://www.keepandbeararms.com

Library of Congress Legislative Information on the Internet
http://thomas.loc.gov

National Institute of Justice
http://www.ojp.usdoj.gov/nij

National Rifle Association
http://www.nra.org

NRA Institute for Legislative Action ("State Gun Laws")
http://nraila.org/GunLaws.asp?FormMode=state

New Yorkers Against Gun Violence
http://www.nyagv.org
Outpost of Freedom
http://www.outpost-of-freedom.com

Remington Arms Co. Inc. Political Action Committee
http://www.rempac.org

Second Amendment Foundation
http://www.saf.org

United Nations Crime and Justice Information Network
http://www.unodc.org/unodc/en/analysis_and_statistics.html

U.S. Department of Justice, Bureau of Justice Statistics
("Firearms and Crime Statistics")
http://www.ojp.usdoj.gov/bjs/guns.htm

U.S. Department of the Treasury, Bureau of Alcohol,
Tobacco, Firearms and Explosives, Statistics Division
("Firearms")
http://www.atf.treas.gov/firearms

Violence Policy Center
http://www.vpc.org/

Web-based Injury Statistics Query and Reporting System
(WISQARS), National Center for Injury Control and
Prevention, Centers for Disease Control
http://www.cdc.gov/ncipc/wisqars/

Bibliography

American Bar Association. "Task Force on Gun Violence, Report to the House of Delegates" (1994).

Congressional Record, 102nd, 103rd, and 106th Congress.

Cook, Philip J., and Jens Ludwig. *Gun Violence: The Real Costs*. Oxford, England: Oxford University Press, 2000.

Cramer, Clayton E. "The Racist Roots of Gun Control," *Kansas Journal of Law and Public Policy* (winter 1995).

The David and Lucile Packard Foundation. "Children, Youth, and Gun Violence," *The Future of Children*, vol. 12, no. 2 (summer/fall 2002).

DeConde, Alexander. *Gun Violence in America: The Struggle for Control.* Boston: Northeastern University Press, 2001.

DeWan, George. "Guns & History," *Newsday,* December. 9, 1993.

Draper, Thomas, ed. *The Issue of Gun Control.* New York: H. W. Wilson Co., 1981.

Eisenhower, Milton, chairman. "Report of the National Commission on the Causes and Prevention of Violence." U.S. Government, December 10, 1969.

Jurist. "Gun Laws, Gun Control & Gun Rights." University of Pittsburgh School of Law http://jurist.law.pitt.edu/index.htm (Accessed April 29, 2003.)

Kellermann, Arthur, et al. "Gun Ownership as a Risk Factor for Homicide in the Home," *The New England Journal of Medicine,* vol. 329, no. 15 (Oct. 7, 1993).

———. "Injuries and deaths due to firearms in the home," *Journal of Trauma,* 45(2) (August 1998).

Kleck, Gary, and Don B. Kates. *Armed: New Perspectives on Gun Control.* New York: Prometheus Books, 2001.

Kluin, Kurt. "Gun Control: Is it a Legal and Effective Means of Controlling Firearms in the United States?" *Washburn Law Journal,* vol. 21 (1982).

Lott, John R. "Concealed guns reduce crime; If people are packing, crooks think twice," *Star Tribune,* Aug. 16, 1998.

Lund, Nelson. "A Primer on the Constitutional Right to Keep and Bear Arms." Virginia Institute for Public Policy report, *Gun Week*, July 20, 2002.

Murray, Iain. "The U.S. Gun-control Debate: A Critical Look." Statistical Assessment Service http://www.stats.org/statswork/index.html (Accessed April 30, 2003.)

Polsby, Daniel D., and Dennis Brennen. "Taking Aim at Gun Control." Heartland policy study, Oct. 30, 1995.

Riczo, Steven. "Guns, America, and the 21st Century," *USA Today* magazine, vol. 129, issue 2670 (March 2001).

Violence Policy Center. "Kids in the Line of Fire: Children, Handguns, and Homicide." November 2001.

———. "Where'd They Get Their Guns? An Analysis of the Firearms Used in High-Profile Shootings, 1963 to 2001." April 2001.

Volokh, Eugene. "Testimony of Eugene Volokh on the Second Amendment." Senate Subcommittee on the Constitution, Sept. 23, 1998.

Yeager, Holly, Evan Moore, and Steve Miletich. "Guns In America," parts 1–4, *Houston Chronicle*, 1997.

Zimring, Franklin E. "Firearms and Federal Law: The Gun Control Act of 1968," *Journal of Legal Studies*, vol. 4 (1975).

Statutes
Articles of Confederation, Article VI
The Bill of Rights

Federal Firearms Act of 1938
Fourteenth Amendment, U.S. Constitution
Gun Control Act of 1968, 18 U.S.C.
Lewis v. *United States*, 445 U.S. 55 (1980)
National Firearms Act of 1934
Pennsylvania Constitution (1790)
Presser v. *State of Illinois*, 116 U.S. 252 (1886)
Quilici v. *Village of Morton Grove*, 695 F.2d 261 (7th Cir. 1982), cert. denied, 464 U.S. 863 (1983)
Rhode Island Constitution
Second Amendment, U.S. Constitution
Tennessee Constitution (1796)
The Uniform Firearms Act
United States v. *Cruikshank*, 92 U.S. 542 (1875), 92 U.S. 542
United States v. *Emerson*. Appeal from the United States District Court for the Northern District of Texas, Oct. 16, 2001
United States v. *Miller*. 307 U.S. (1939)
United States v. *Oakes*, 564 F.2d 384 (10th Circuit 1977)
Virginia Constitution (1776)

Index

Page numbers in **boldface** are illustrations.

About the Author

Susan Dudley Gold has written more than two dozen books for children and teens on a variety of topics, including American history, health issues, law, and space. She has also written several books on Maine history. Among her many careers in journalism are stints as a reporter for a daily newspaper, managing editor of two statewide business magazines, and freelance writer for several regional publications. Susan has received numerous awards for her writing and design work. She and her husband, John Gold, also a children's book author, live in Maine. They have one son, Samuel.